MOTHERS DON'T

KATIXA
AGIRRE
MOTHERS
DON'T

Translated from Basque by Kristin Addis

3TimesRebel

First published by 3TimesRebel Press in 2022, our first year of existence.

Title: *Mothers Don't* by Katixa Agirre
Original title: *Amek ez dute* Copyright © Katixa Agirre, 2018
Originally published by Elkar Argitaletxea
Copyright © Publication by arrangement with Open Letter Books, New York

Translation from Basque: Copyright © Kristin Addis, 2022

Design and layout: Enric Jardí

Illustrations: Anna Pont Armengol

Editing and proof reading: Greg Mulhern, Carme Bou, Bibiana Mas

Maria-Mercè Marçal's poem *Deriva*:
© heiresses of Maria-Mercè Marçal

Translation of Maria-Mercè Marçal's poem *Deriva*:
© Dr Sam Abrams

Author photograph: © Zaloa Fuertes

Printed and bound by TJ Books, Padstow, Cornwall, England
Paperback ISBN: 978-1-7398236-0-3
eBook ISBN: 978-1-7398236-4-1

www.3timesrebel.com

PART I
CREATION

PART 1
CREATION

1

THE REVELATION

And amongst mortals I do assert
that they who are wholly without
experience and have never had
children far surpass in happiness
those who are parents.
EURIPIDES, *MEDEA*

IT HAPPENED IN THE MIDDLE OF SUMMER.

On a Thursday afternoon.

That day, the nanny walked through the gates of the house in Armentia as if she were opening the doors to hell: cheeks red and reluctantly. As usual, she felt that her time off, four hours on Thursday afternoons, had gone by quickly, too quickly. The girl's name was Mélanie, and she had been in Gasteiz for nine months, learning Spanish and trying to decide what her next step in life should be. She locked her bike in the back garden, tried to brush the mud off her sandals, and entered the house uneasily. She didn't hear a sound. She peeked cautiously into the kitchen, the living room, and the room that the lady of the house used as a studio. She was thinking about the boy she had met that day, who had invited her on a bike ride through Salburua Park. He wasn't too bad.

She didn't announce her arrival or call out her employer's name, she trod softly in case the twins were sleeping – she didn't suppose they would be fast asleep at that hour of the afternoon, but she could hope. The children were very light sleepers, as she knew all too well by now. But, if by some miracle the children were asleep, perhaps she would have time for a shower before going back to work. What a sweet idea that was! She had mud on her ankles and on her blue shorts. When she had lain down in the grass with the new boy, she hadn't noticed how wet the ground was.

Sandals off, she went up the carpeted stairs to the next floor. There, on the top step, she felt an ominous vibration that she would surely have immediately forgotten about, if it hadn't been for what happened next. She would later describe it as an impulse to flee: she saw herself flying down San Prudentzio Avenue on her bicycle, free, never looking back. It wasn't the first time she had felt such an impulse since she had come to live in that house, but she did not obey it this time either. How could she? Instead, she went on down the hall, heart pounding. She came to her employers' bedroom. The door was open. She was holding her breath. She peered inside and saw two lumps, like little bundles, on the parents' bed; half hidden by the duvet, only their heads were visible. It was the twins, both with their eyes closed. In an armchair next to them, she saw the mother, Alice Espanet, wearing nothing but a nightgown, one breast exposed. The left one.

The nanny, a twenty-two-year-old au pair from Orléans, a pretty girl and, until that moment, a happy one, said nothing, or at least can't recall if she did. She moved closer, trembling. And as she took those five steps forward, her mind went blank. She didn't, couldn't, look at the mother. She felt empty, erased, evaporated, removed, for the first time in her short life.

She barely touched the little bundles. Half a second was enough. The twins were not moving but they were not asleep. Purple lips and cold skin. Both naked. The sheet still wet.

'They're fine now,' said the mother, calmly, but Mélanie jumped at the sound of her voice: a terrible, unbearable sound.

But even more terrifying than the mother's voice was her demeanour; she was indifferent, composed, unperturbed.

Mélanie grabbed the phone from the night table – she doesn't remember doing it, but she must have – the same phone she used to call France whenever she was alone in the house (which was not often, unfortunately). This time, however, she called, distressed, for an ambulance, the police, anyone, begging in her meagre Spanish. It was a two-minute call full of sighs, incomprehensible details and disbelief, and Alice Espanet remained calm the whole time. She neither rose from her chair nor bothered to cover her breast.

Somehow the recipient of the call understood and believed her, and after a short while, which felt like an eternity, the house in Armentia began to fill with people. The house was a sturdy yet discreet villa, bought three years earlier, after a bitter dispute with the architect. Mélanie was waiting outside when the chaos descended, hugging her knees and shivering on the front steps, examining again the mud on her shoes. They brought her into the kitchen and sat her down. They asked her questions and she tried to answer them. 'Mélanie, tell us what happened, take all the time you need ...' But she couldn't stop crying and her neck felt tight and she could barely breathe, never mind speak. Someone brought her a glass of water, and someone else gave her a small white pill. She swallowed it without asking what it was.

For several hours, the ambulances and police cars shone coloured lights across the front of the elegant house; from a distance it looked like some sort of grand opening, and more than a few neighbours came over to see what was going on, as well as cheerful passersby and even a few disciplined joggers out for a late run. It was a warm, sweet summer evening, rare in Gasteiz, perfect for outdoor activities. No one but Mélanie wanted to go home, and the rumours grew, becoming more and more harrowing.

The father, Ricardo to his clients, Ritxi to his friends, got home ten minutes before the inspector arrived, the day's sheen of sweat still drying on his skin. He had just left Madrid in a chauffeured rental car when Mélanie had ended her afternoon off and entered the house in her muddied sandals. He immediately saw the twins' small bodies being put into huge grey body bags. Then he watched his wife being put in the back of a police car, in the sports clothes she usually wore to Pilates (black leggings and a loose Mango t-shirt). She was not handcuffed. Absurdly, Ritxi found this comforting. He called her name, once, but she didn't even turn her head to look at him. She sat in the car with her head held high; a Eurydice of salt.

He was told the name of a hospital. Seventh floor. Psychiatric Evaluation.

He was also offered a tiny white pill, but he turned it down, perhaps batting it away to remain forever hidden under the sofa.

No one saw him cry.

The nanny, who had been living in a small upstairs room with a big window, asked him if she could go to a friend's house for the night. The man of the house answered with nothing more than a barely perceptible wave of his hand, and Mélanie prepared to flee at last on her bike, never to return. But the police wouldn't let her go, and she spent a long evening being questioned at the station, until in the end she had no more tears left to cry. Then, finally, she was allowed her bicycle. Not long afterwards she left the country for Paris and tried to find work as an actress for a while. Fourteen months later she had a panic attack when she was told she would have to testify at the trial.

Ritxi's parents had passed away, his only brother was living in the States, and he hotly refused all help offered by on-call psychologists and well-meaning friends. He wanted to stay in the house, and he needed to be alone. He was so insistent that finally, just after midnight, they left him to it. Instead of taking him straight to the police station, they let him wait until the morning.

He disconnected all the phones.

The next morning, at the stroke of eight, two police officers arrived at the house in Armentia, where an apparently calm Ritxi – *too calm, if you ask me*, one of the officers said later – opened the American red oak front door. They said they were terribly sorry, but Ritxi was needed at the police station, and they couldn't wait any longer. They had to ask him some questions. Ritxi asked them for two minutes to change his shirt – he was still wearing the one from the night before, stained and sweaty from Madrid – and invited them in while he went upstairs.

He was as good as his word and soon they were on their way.

THE NEWS HAD BROKEN TOO LATE FOR THE EDITORIAL OFFICES to get it into the evening reports, but it was in all the head-lines the following day. It was summer and the media chewed on the story over and over again, until it became the only item on the agenda. In this second decade of the 21st century, homicide is a rarity among us, an act reserved for husbands or ex-husbands to commit, infrequently, against their wives or ex-wives. *The inevitable minimum*, it seems. This is why certain homicides guarantee ratings and mouse-clicks, espe-cially those that don't involve a husband or ex-husband.

The uproar also reached me, of course. I did everything I could to ignore the incident, however: changed the channel, turned the page, closed the window. If anyone mentioned it to me, I would just change the subject and talk about the stifling heat. It was truly unbearable that summer, so damned hot the whole time.

Most people knew not to talk about it in front of me. However, there are always a few thoughtless people, at the butcher's, at the hairdresser's, at weddings, everywhere really.

It was too much for me, under the circumstances. I didn't know how to deal with the incident, and I didn't want to deal with it anyway. It was an active and conscious effort and, though it took a lot of energy on my part, I thought I was handling the challenge well.

But then, exactly two weeks later, things changed dramatically.

Two weeks after Alice Espanet killed her twins – allegedly – the incident was nothing more than a grey gooey memory in the media and the consciousness of good citizens. In front of the house in Armentia, the flowers left by those good citizens were starting to wilt, and the teddy bears were growing mould. I, however, was far away: trapped in the newly opened Obstetric Functional Unit of Basurto Hospital, starting to feel the first contractions brought on by the prostaglandin tampon.

My induced labour had just started and I was hooked up to a monitor, waiting for unimaginable pain to begin or, in psychoanalyst Helene Deutsch's words, 'an orgy of masochistic pleasure'.

In my case, I felt no pleasure, no masochism, and – if I have to say so – certainly no orgy.

I did, however, have a revelation. A revelation that would come to determine the course of my life, or – with honest deference to the child whom I was about to bring into the world – at least the next two or three years of it.

It is not clear what function the pain of contractions actually serves: some say it's a Biblical curse; others that it's inflicted psychologically by a misogynistic society. Strictly speaking, the physiology of childbirth remains a mystery to medical science, as is often the case with issues that pertain only to women. According to some, this particular kind of pain is the only way to access the paleocortex, that is, our primitive brain. Over the millennia, we have added many layers of reasoning to our primitive brain: the modern part of the brain is called the neocortex, and the rational participation of the neocortex makes it impossible to give birth, apparently. We need to revert to our reptilian instinct, to return to the jungle, forget that we can communicate through articulated language and walk on two legs: on a fundamental level, it is only by forgetting evolution, by travelling backwards millions of years, that we are able to give birth. So this is the function of the pain then: to knock out the neocortex, to paralyse it, so that we can feel like a powerful gorilla giving birth in the deepest heart of Africa.

This may explain why I reacted so negatively when the midwife first offered me an epidural. She would have dragged me out of the jungle with the anaesthesia. She was a sweet woman, really; she called me *hon*.

'You've worked hard, *hon*, you're fully effaced and three centimetres dilated. We can take you down for the epidural whenever you want.'

'No, fuck no!'

As I said, I was a gorilla in the jungle.

You can't talk to gorillas.

Speech belongs to the realm of the neocortex.

I expect that, as a professional, she wouldn't have taken it the wrong way and, to be honest, I'm not ashamed of swearing at her; I blame it on the paleocortex, and what happened next. Three contractions later, I felt indescribable pain, pain that sent me hurtling into another dimension, to another place and another city and another planet, and even another era (I saw torches instead of lamps, and Roman togas instead of doctors' lab coats, I really did), and that's when I had THE REVELATION.

I had met her eleven years before, Alice Espanet, the – allegedly – insane and ruthless murderer. Of course I had!

And not only that, but we lived right next door to each other for a week or so, back before she was known as Alice Espanet. This is what came to me, with startling clarity, while I was swept up in my whirlwind of pain. Because I had ignored the images in the media, because I hadn't even thought about her since the time I knew her, which would have been eleven years ago, I almost didn't recognise her. But, thanks to the collusion of prostaglandin and oxytocin, thanks to the atavistic capacity of the paleocortex in fact, the truth was suddenly revealed to me: I had once known this – allegedly – evil woman, back when I was young and naive and knew nothing of pain.

BUT, IN ORDER TO ENDURE CONTRACTIONS WITH DIGNITY, YOU must maintain control over your breath. They teach this in every single antenatal class. Follow the rhythm: breathe in, one, two, breathe out, one, two, three, four. If you lose the rhythm, you're done for. The pain then takes control of you and lashes you with its briars. It has its way with you. You lose all self-confidence. You're no longer a gorilla, you're just a rag doll.

I had to ask for the epidural in the end, since I'd lost my concentration with THE REVELATION. The midwife who called me *hon* had finished her shift by then, thank goodness.

While the anaesthetic was taking effect, I commanded myself to hang onto THE REVELATION. I don't know why I thought the epidural had amnesiac powers. It doesn't. I managed to remember everything.

Seven hours later, Erik was born. He was so small, four and a half pounds of warmth and mess. They placed him on my chest, where he left a small brownish splotch the shape of Lanzarote. All I remember from that moment is confusion, noise and disbelief. They took him away immediately, and suddenly the delivery room was full of people – they may have been there before – all rushing about. While I stroked the empty space where my baby had been, they mentioned Apgar tests and meconium stains by way of an explanation. What they meant to say was that I wouldn't have my baby back any time soon. Even though, in the final weeks of my pregnancy, they had diagnosed him as SGA, the gynae-cologist who decided to induce me wrote IUGR in my file. The meanings of these acronyms are no longer relevant; I'll just say that IUGR is worse than SGA: if SGA means that the baby is *small*, IUGR means that he's *too small*. Hence the sudden need to get him out of me. However, they assured me that all would be fine before sending me to the Obstetric Functional Unit with a rather slender hospital attendant. I was 38 weeks gone, the pregnancy could therefore be con-sidered full term, and they could wrap things up.

'Don't worry, often we don't even have to put them in an incubator,' said the doctor, after writing SGA in my file in large letters.

And the doctor was not wrong. They didn't put him in an incubator, but he did spend eight hours in the NICU, away from me. With his four and a half pounds of warmth and mess, he was the biggest baby there, according to Niclas, who visited a couple of times and took pictures. They wouldn't let me go because I was still under the effects of the epidural.

Niclas came back to see me, excited but worried. He kept saying, 'believe it or not, he's the biggest one in there, he really is,' and he zoomed in on the pictures to examine every little detail, while all I could say was that I was tired and could he please leave me alone. However, even though I was truly exhausted, I couldn't fall asleep. I turned onto my side in the hospital bed, but all I could think of was Alice Espanet, who had gone by the name Jade when I knew her. Perhaps it was just a coping strategy to avoid thinking about Erik, to trick myself into believing everything would be fine. From time to time, I looked at the Lanzarote-shaped mark and even brought my nose to it to inhale its sweet scent.

Finally, at dusk, they brought him back to me. He had been cleaned up, but still had the sharp, sweet smell I remembered. A little bun, fresh out of the oven. I just wanted to eat him all up! Literally.

They explained all the tests and analyses they had performed on Erik – he had plasters on his tiny thighs to prove it – but I didn't understand a thing they said. I just wanted to hear that everything was fine, and told them I didn't need to know anything else. Yes, he was small, and no, they didn't know why. *Pregnancy is still largely a mystery*, the paediatrician openly admitted. Erik had stopped gaining weight while he was inside my belly; in fact, he may have even lost weight over the last few days, so he was better off out, where he would surely now gain weight, no problem, and SGA, and IUGR, and percentiles, and … just leave me alone already.

Trying to follow the midwife's confusing instructions, I held the baby to my breast, and this, more or less, became my sole duty for the next several months. I turned into a pair of tits on legs, attached to a child.

THAT WAS THE VIEW FROM OUTSIDE, ANYWAY. BUT ON THE inside, my situation was quite different and increasingly difficult. I had stitches between my legs – just a first-degree tear, but painful nonetheless, as were my nipples – and how! I had a hemorrhoid for the first time in my life, my muscles were still sore from the enormous exertion of the final half hour of labour, and I was frailer than an autumn leaf due to as yet undiagnosed anaemia. On top of all this, I couldn't sleep. Or at least it seemed that way to me: sleep called to me now and then, but I never sank into it as deeply as I needed to, and I would never know that simple pleasure again.

I was in constant pain, but could find no use for it. Beyond the borders of the pain, however, I couldn't get Jade/Alice out of my mind. And I knew I had no choice but to embrace my obsession. I'm a writer, after all, and that is a writer's sole mandate.

When you're exhausted, utterly destroyed, it's a lot easier to give in to your obsessions. You are entirely at their mercy.

This is why I had to write to Léa the moment I got home and had a free hand. I had met Léa eleven years earlier. We lived together for a year when we were students, and have kept in touch ever since, despite the distance between us. First we emailed each other, then we exchanged loads of Facebook messages, comments and likes. In the final weeks of my pregnancy we turned to Telegram, at Léa's suggestion.

It was through this third platform that I sent her a picture of Erik but, unlike other mothers, I didn't include his weight or any other details. It was plainly obvious that he was tiny.

Erik has arrived, all is well! was all I wrote.

A message of congratulations and a long row of heart emojis came back immediately. The phone danced with messages for a while. She asked me how I was doing, if it had been difficult. I told her it hadn't, without going into any detail. Then the phone went quiet. It was time for the message that would reveal the actual reason for my communication. I took a moment to find the right words.

I heard about Jade.

Silence.

Had some task come up that prevented her from reading my message? Was she at a loss for words, silenced by the grimness of the incident? Or perhaps she hadn't heard about it – after all, it had happened on the other side of the border, and Léa had long since lost contact with the woman, Jade no longer used the name Jade, etc., etc. ... – maybe she didn't know how to respond without further explanation?

Silence.

It was the first time I had spoken about the case with anyone. To let my obsession gestate properly, I hadn't wanted to talk it over with anyone until now. Not even with Niclas. But now Léa, my chosen and much needed confidante, was cruelly letting me down. This couldn't be happening! Riddled with anxiety, I switched Erik to the other breast without knowing if he was ready. There were no new messages.

I kept waiting; I had no other purpose in life.

The baby suckled.

I resigned myself to the pain in my nipples.

Then the phone pinged.

How did you find out?

So she did know. The news had reached Avignon. Of course it had. A French woman drowns her twins in Spain; of course it would have been reported. An incomprehensible murder. Profiles of Jade/Alice. All the gory details. Recollections from the neighbours of her youth. The media had to have all the juicy details there too.

I quickly explained that it had all happened not far from where I lived, only 40 miles away (I knew well enough that geography wasn't Léa's strong point; the first time I mentioned Bilbao to her, she asked me if it was in Portugal), and that the news had made quite a splash.

We're in shock. I don't know what to say.

She meant it literally and seemed to have nothing else to add. Erik moved his head away (his way of saying he didn't want to breastfeed any more) and, after doing up my nursing bra, I placed him on my shoulder to walk up and down the hall for our usual 'fart parade'.

Léa was quite the talker. She had been a talker when I first met her at the university in England, and continued to be throughout our long-distance relationship as well. Now, however, she was leaving me hanging, neither understanding nor satisfying my thirst for information. Should I send her another message to give her a little nudge?

Of course I should.

I can imagine. We'll talk more another time. Xoxo.

I signed off, but wanted to leave the door open (another time = as soon as possible please) and finished the 'fart parade' faster than usual. Erik understood to some extent that I was upset, passed his gas quickly, and then fell asleep. A twelve-minute nap.

IT HAPPENED IN THE HEART OF ENGLAND, THE MIDLANDS. THE university was small and had been founded fairly recently, after the boom that came as a result of a change in the law in the early 90s. It specialised in sports, business and communication. The faculty members' offices were located in two pavilions that had been used as a hospital in World War II. The ghostly wails of amputees can still be heard there, if you listen closely enough. Our lifestyle revolved around the campus – we lived in a dorm on campus, got drunk at the campus disco, and cleaned it all up in the morning for £4.50 an hour – and we were happy, in a simple way.

I arrived on the 8th of September and Léa arrived on the 9th. We lived across the hall from each other. I lived in Apartment A and she was in Apartment B. We kept the doors of the two apartments open constantly, using fire extinguishers as doorstops, so it felt like we lived in a single large 'Apartment A/B'. There was always something going on in our hall. We also used to leave our bedroom doors open, in case an opportunity – any opportunity – might arise. It was impossible to be alone, but we – I, at least – never missed solitude. I remember that period as a time of laughter, tears and indiscreet promiscuity; an intensely enjoyable time of my life.

Léa didn't arrive alone. She brought a friend with her the first week, to help her settle in. Léa brought a lot of luggage, and she needed a porter.

The porter's name was Jade.

I didn't pay much attention to the two French girls in that first week, and even less when I found out that Jade wasn't even a student. I was new to the campus, to the city, to the country. I was looking for people who I could be friends with for the whole year and didn't care about anyone who was only staying there for a week. You need to prioritise where you focus your energy in a foreign country; especially if you don't speak the language well. Jade's beauty always attracted attention – she had cat eyes – but she wasn't particularly friendly and it was very difficult to understand her English. She said *Aye!* for *Hi!*, for example. I only remember her being in two places: in the hallway between Apartments A and B, half hidden behind Léa, and at one of the early parties, in Apartment C if I'm not mistaken; awkward smile on her face, plastic cup in hand, surrounded by a pack of boys of varying nationalities. Other than these two images of her, I don't remember a thing.

I had been digging through my mind for memories of Jade since the day of THE REVELATION, but the mine was empty now, apparently. Her *Aye!* and her cat eyes. That would have to do for now. She was just a woman, one who had left no major impression on me. Too bad. But what else was I expecting? That all of a sudden I would remember that I had spotted a malevolent spark in 21-year-old Jade's eye, and that, by tracing the path of history backwards, everything would make sense: our meeting, her misdeeds, the dead children, and the rest of it? Of course not. So why did I feel so bad?

During a twenty-minute nap the afternoon of the day of my conversation with Léa, I dreamt I was in the hallway between Apartments A and B. In the dream, Erik was hanging from one of my breasts, the right one, and Jade, also hungry, was trying to suckle from the left. I kept hitting her on the forehead with a spoon, telling her to leave me alone. But I said it in French, *Fiche-moi la paix, putain!* even though I don't know any French.

Although I don't usually pay much attention to dreams, this case of xenoglossia upset me for quite a while.

2
THE DECISION

Mothers don't write, they are written.
SUSAN SULEIMAN

IN THE AUTUMN OF THE SAME YEAR, WHEN MOTHERHOOD HAD physically and psychologically sucked me dry and I had finally (and at an irreversible cost to my nipples) managed to get Erik into the 3rd percentile – or, more specifically, he had edged into the realm of normalcy – something truly unexpected happened.

The phone rang, interrupting our usual twenty-minute morning nap. I answered hotly, expecting it to be a Latinx telemarketer since, at that point, no one called me voluntarily (no one wanted to bother me, they said, since I must surely be busy). Instead, someone from the Basque Government spoke to me apprehensively on the other end of the line. They wanted to give me a prize. The Euskadi Award. I stared at the phone, then put it back to my ear and snapped, 'Yeah, right!'

Fortunately, the voice on the other end of the line took little notice and started to explain the process they went through each year. If I accepted the prize, I would have to give a press conference, and go to a ceremony a few weeks later, where I would be expected to say a few words ... Photos ... The President and Deputy Minister of the Basque Country ... A small banquet, then home with a big smile on my face.

It would take place in Gasteiz.

'But for which book?'

The civil servant didn't answer that either, thank goodness. It was a stupid question since I had only one book: a true-crime political thriller that had been published a year and a half earlier. But just then Erik started to cry, saving me from the situation, and I hung up, promising to call back later. Could this really be happening? Still holding the baby, I googled the telephone number and it really was a number from the Ministry of Culture. Well, hell! So it was true. Should I jump up and down? Would I hurt my pelvic floor if I did?

The book follows the final steps of ETA's only victim from the United States and, in a parallel storyline, follows the movements of the three members of the Madrid cell that killed him. It opens in an attractive, suburban, middle-class neighbourhood in New Jersey, where Eugene Kenneth Brown (Gene to his friends and family), an inventory specialist for Johnson & Johnson, is saying goodbye to his wife and children. He sets off for Newark Airport with nothing but a small suitcase. On the same day, someone steals a Peugeot 505 from the Amara neighbourhood in Donostia. The Peugeot, with a newly-fitted fake licence plate, then moves on to Madrid.

Gene arrives in Madrid. So does the Peugeot. The reader is then introduced to two men and a woman, who are in an apartment in Madrid. They are manufacturing a bomb for the car, which they will park on Carbonero y Sol Street. The two men and the woman are referred to by their real names, since the three of them became quite well known after the event. One of the men was publically known because, in a fit of remorse, he confessed all the details of this attack and several others; the other man because, as he was about to leave jail, a new sentence was clumsily fabricated, leading to hunger strikes and a number of other protests; and the woman, because she was a leading figure in the peace negotiations in Algeria and Switzerland, in 1989 and 1999.

In a tonal shift, the last third of the book is graphically violent. There's an explosion, but it doesn't kill all the Civil Guards who were the intended targets of the attack. To complete their mission, the members of ETA open fire on the already wounded Civil Guards, but they are all dreadful shots. Reinforcements arrive, other Civil Guards on duty at the nearby Soviet embassy, and they join the shooting. It's a harsh passage, hyperrealistic and inspired by war reporting. When the hail of bullets finally falls silent and the smoke clears, there's a single body in the middle of the chaos: Johnson & Johnson's inventory specialist Eugene Kenneth Brown, from the U.S., still wearing his trainers. It was seven in the morning and he had wanted to stretch his legs a bit before getting on the plane back to Newark.

All sorts of things were said about my novel, *Inventory*: that it whitewashed ETA's crimes by portraying its members as ordinary people (who ate strawberries, took showers, and were sexually repressed), that I had bought into and was spreading all the war propaganda against the Madrid cell, that I was more understanding towards the female character just because I was a woman, that I was dragging the good name of the woman, who had been so important in peace talks, through the mud, that I was exploiting people's morbid curiosity, that I wasn't taking the victims into account, that I didn't talk about the torture inflicted by the Civil Guards, that I was a parasite of the Basque conflict, sucking everything I could out of it while it was still a hot topic.

In any case, there was no denying that the minor controversy had been good for the book, which was in its 7th edition after only a year and a half in print. This commercial success infuriated professionals and amateurs alike – truly awful things were said about me on Twitter (which I took badly at first), but this simply increased sales, which took off in a way that was a delight to witness. Soon after, the book was translated into Spanish, published by a small, semi-hipster press in Barcelona, and then things got even better. A leftist representative from Madrid praised the book on Twitter and other representatives then questioned whether he was a friend to the terrorists or not. Sales of the book hit an all-time high. It was translated into Catalan and Hungarian not long after, and was expected to be published in Polish soon as well. My agent was even about to sign a deal for an English translation (the holy grail!). Then came the possibility of a film adaptation, which has not yet materialised but, while we wait for the funding to be confirmed, I am required to renew a contract every year in which I basically sacrifice my publishing rights for pennies. I was busy in those days. I was invited to speak in the most elegant auditoriums in the Basque Country. I was also offered the floor in Madrid, in Barcelona, in a small but well-kept bookshop in Menorca, in

Liverpool at a university seminar on Basque literature. I had to pass on the Frankfurt Book Fair, for reasons of motherhood: Erik was still a newborn back then. I was given the 111 Academy Award too, which is decided by a readers' vote. I saw pictures of myself, repeatedly printed in the pages of the newspapers, even on the front page a few times. Every time a famous cultural figure died, I was asked for a few words of praise, to be published in the papers.

When I think back to that unexpected, whirlwind period, it seems like another lifetime, a time when we used torches instead of lamps and Roman togas instead of lab coats.

So I didn't jump for joy. I was perturbed for a good half hour. I took the baby in my arms and laid him in his cot again. He was asleep now, but I still didn't dare call the Basque Government back. Why was I so unsettled? The reason I felt so uncomfortable was that, for me, the book was a thing of the past. So much so that, at this point it didn't even feel like it was mine. And what's more, the thought that at one time it had been the centre of my life felt profoundly embarrassing. And now – now! – they wanted to give me a prize, and the most important prize in Basque writing besides. It was all utterly absurd.

Back then, when the book had first started to appear in bookshop windows, I would cross the street to look at people's expressions, hoping to see whether they could tell that I was the one who had written *Inventory*. It had to be obvious, right? Surely they could tell from my face that I was THE AUTHOR, right? I felt different at work too and, even though they tried to hide it, I'm sure everyone there looked at me differently. I would go over to the coffee machine with a smug grin on my face, greeting my co-workers with an air of obnoxious arrogance; after all, *I* was the author of *Inventory* and they weren't.

A similar thing happens to young people the first time they get laid. They don't realise that their faces tell the whole story.

Later I realised that nobody – except for contemptuous critics, of course – even cared whether or not I was the THE AUTHOR of *Inventory*. I made a much bigger impression wherever I went – at work, in the shops, on the tube, with friends – once my baby bump began to show. Now that was emotion and commotion!

This was surely the result of our ridiculously low birth rate, whereas books multiply like rabbits; they're out of control.

A few months later, once I had become a mother, everything had changed, and when I went out alone – which happened rarely – my feelings were very different. No arrogance, no smugness. On the contrary, I felt naked, incomplete, an inadvertent fraud. I felt an urge to explain myself to every passer-by: *wait, just a minute, I'm not really like this, something's missing here, I'm a mother, you understand? You see me like this, all alone on the street, but you can't possibly understand me like this!* From time to time, I did feel a need to be free of the baby, but whenever I left him to go for a walk by myself, it was worse; the baby's absence constantly weighed heavily on my conscience.

After three months without managing to sleep more than three hours in a row, after taking the baby to be weighed every other day at first, then once a week, then once every two weeks, after keeping detailed records of the baby's every poop/puke/snot/cough, my identity as a mother had swallowed up all other identities, condemning all my previous selves to utter oblivion. A writer? Me? A worker? Me? A wife? A daughter? A friend? Someone who had waded naked in the fountain in Trafalgar Square? Who used to hook up with American tourists, one summer when I was a guide at Loch Ness? Me? Yeah, right!

The call from the Basque Government made me sit up and take notice. I was no longer myself. And once I got over my initial confusion, I made a decision: it was time for the tides to turn. I would have to start picking up the pieces of my shattered self, wherever they might be. I could think of only one way to do that.

I WAITED TWO OR THREE DAYS BEFORE TELLING NICLAS ABOUT my decision so he wouldn't think it was just a foolish whim. We celebrated the prize, and I even drank a bit of cava, though as a diligent breast-feeder, this never sat right with my conscience. Niclas couldn't understand how much the news had shaken me up. A prize, okay, but it wasn't the first. And the money was nice, no doubt about that, but it wasn't exactly enough to change our lives.

I told him one bath time, since that was generally a relaxed time for all three of us. With the eighteen thousand euros in prize money (*don't forget about tax*, said Niclas, obsessed with taxes, as always), I was going to apply for a leave of absence, starting in February. The 1st of February, that was the day we circled in red, since that was the day my maternity leave would end, plus all the hours I'd accumulated for breastfeeding, plus my whole year's holiday time. We were heading for *terra incognita*; I was supposed to return to normal life with this scar between my legs, as if nothing had happened down there.

Niclas' eyes widened. He was upset, much more upset than I was, at the thought of sending our baby to the nursery at only six months old: nothing of the sort would ever happen in Sweden. But then he started to say he thought it was a great idea, that he had been thinking along the same lines but hadn't dared to bring it up ... And, now that he thought about it, he could be the one to take a leave of absence, it would be no bad thing for me to go back to work, he knew staying at home for six months hadn't been easy for me. I had to stop him right there.

'No, Niclas. I want to take the leave of absence. And Erik will go to the nursery in February.'

His expression made it clear that he didn't understand because of our cultural differences.

'I'm taking the leave to write.'

As a child of the most feminist country in the world (or so they think, at least), Niclas said nothing, but went pale. He was still pale as we sat down to dinner once the baby was asleep. I tried to smooth things over, for myself as well as for him.

'It'll only be four hours, from nine to one, not the seven hours we thought about at first. Since he naps in the morning, he'll hardly even notice.'

I kept talking about the nursery. About how it had made such a good impression on us when we'd had a look round.

About Montessori and Pickler and their respectful approaches towards children; all of which was taken very seriously by the nursery. Niclas told me he understood. He said he had never stood in the way of my literary career and he wasn't going to start now. For a minute, I thought he would remind me of the holiday we'd taken to New Jersey when I was researching my book. But he didn't mention New Jersey. I couldn't believe it. It's not easy being the husband of a writer. No one would choose to be, it just happens. He finished his omelette quickly, took a final swig of his beer, and asked the million-dollar question.

'So, what are you going to write about? Do you have an idea?'

I answered him calmly, lightly, so that the need, the urgency, the obsession that lurked behind my words wouldn't betray itself.

'I want to write about that woman. You know, the mother who killed her children last summer, remember her?'

BOOKKEEPING FOR THE *MATER FAMILIAS* AND WRITER.

Average monthly expenses:

√ Rent: €730.

√ Electricity: €55.

√ Gas: €90.

√ Telephones (landline and mobile) and internet: €90.

√ Nursery: €190.

√ Groceries and general purchases: €300.

√ Nappies (generic): €80.

√ Car expenses: €150.

√ Newspaper and media subscriptions: €40.

√ Contributions to NGOs: €50.

√ Miscellaneous: €200.

€1,975 a month. Suddenly it seemed like a tremendous amount, unmanageable, and I didn't know how to make cutbacks, except to the detriment of the Palestinian refugees. This meant that on top of the €1,200 that Niclas received from the academy, I would have to add €775 at least, if we were to maintain our current lifestyle, whose only luxury was the baby's organic cereal.

AT WORK, I SAID NOTHING ABOUT MY BOOK PROJECT, OF course. Officially, I was a good mother and I was taking a leave of absence to take care of my child. No one dared challenge me. In terms of paperwork, it's much more complicated to reduce your hours than to take an entire leave of absence. I had heard my boss say it many times. They signed the paperwork I needed, gave Erik an affectionate pat or two in the baby carrier, and I was free. Or as free as a mother ever can be, anyway.

I still had one more test to pass, however: leaving the baby at the nursery. We had to make the adjustment over a period of two weeks. Instead of jumping head first into a freezing cold pool, like we did when we were young, now the accepted protocol was to test the water first with one foot and then the other, then to go in up to your knees, then your waist, and finally ... splash! That was adaptation. On the first day,

I stayed with the baby in the classroom for half an hour. The next day, I went out into the hall for twenty minutes, leaving him in the classroom. On the third day, I waited at the café across the street for forty minutes.

From the fourth day onwards, I brought my laptop with me. I carried Erik on my front in his baby carrier and my laptop in a backpack on my back. By the time most of the mothers – and the odd father – had left the classroom struggling to hold back their tears, I was sitting at the biggest table in the café with my laptop in front of me. Sometimes a couple of mothers who had recently become friends thanks to the nursery sat at the table next to mine, enjoying a bit of social life. They looked at me curiously, while I tried not to return their gaze. I didn't have a single minute to waste.

I got to work eagerly. During those first two weeks of adaptation, I figured out how best to start my investigation. I made lists, identified sources, decided where I would begin and end Jade/Alice's story. I made a list of places I had to visit. I debated with myself how far I was prepared to go. Would I be a lawyer for the defence or the prosecution? What did I want to be? Was it the writer's job to be the judge? Or was that task better left to the reader? Was it acceptable to use fiction, or should I tell the story as it actually happened, in a factual, journalistic style, without attempting to shine a light on what I did not and could never know?

And, critically, if I decided against the journalistic approach, what style would I adopt? Was it even possible to stylise this most heinous of crimes: violence against children? The question made me shudder, so I set it aside for the time being.

What to do about names, dates, specific details? Would I have to change them for moral, legal or literary reasons? And then, there was the question that had been niggling at me from the start: should I get in touch with Jade/Alice? Maybe write her a letter, like that French writer who wrote to the man that had murdered his whole family? Try to arrange an in-person interview with her, perhaps? Leaving aside my own inclinations regarding the issue – which were ambivalent at most, and therefore not helpful in the least – did the book really need that or, alternatively, could it wreak irreparable damage, a toxic contamination that might, in the end, accomplish nothing except a disastrous diversion? Even if such a meeting were possible – and I had my doubts – how much did I stand to gain from it, and how much could I lose?

These were the lists, the questions, the doubts I typed on my keyboard while Erik was adapting to daycare. Occasionally, someone called from a local magazine or radio station, the last round of interviews from the prize. Then, when the mothers at the next table got up to leave, I gathered my things together, turned my laptop off, washed my hands, and went over to hug my little Viking and cover him in kisses before putting him in the baby carrier and taking him home.

I feel nostalgic now, for those early days when the book was no more than a bright, shining idea full of promise.

3
NATURAL KILLERS

Houses belong to the neighbours,
countries, to foreigners,
and children, to women
who never wanted children.
ANA MARTINS MARQUES

THE CLINIC IS JUST OFF THE MOTORWAY THAT RUNS BETWEEN Erandio and Sopela, on the right as you drive towards the coast. Traffic tends to bottleneck there, but there's always parking spaces around the back. The building looks new, with its façade of rain-washed glass, and the sign announcing its services goes mostly unnoticed by drivers.

This is where it all began.

Ritxi and Alice came here twenty-one times. From their initial concerns to their final success. A two and a half-year journey. They would make a day out of their visits, trying to keep their hopes up. Ritxi was better at this, his optimism seemed boundless. At the clinic he was compliant, the model patient. Alice's moods would change from day to day. She could be on top of the world one day, and down in the dumps the next. Never in between. And on the whole, she was not very talkative.

When Ritxi's work allowed, they would take the rest of the day off after the appointment and go out for a nice lunch somewhere. To the coast, if the weather was good, to Pobeña or the old port town of Algorta. In the winter, they preferred to go into Bilbo. Their favourite place was a one-star restaurant on the Marzana quay. Alice had given up alcohol and was trying to eat 'cleanly,' but she was always able to find a suitable dish there.

If nothing happens after trying the traditional way for a year, that's when alarm bells start ringing. Alice and Ritxi didn't wait that long. Ritxi in particular was starting to feel old and pressed for time. And he was not used to losing. After seven months of failure, they came to this highly recommended clinic, hoping to end the obstacles to their parenthood.

So, this is where it all began.

In this clinic, in this waiting room painted in pastel shades. Blood tests and sperm counts, karyotype analysis and ultrasounds, primrose oil and folic acid, all those hormones that lurk behind the acronyms (FSH, LT, AMH), gynaecologists, endocrinologists, haematologists, hysterosalpingography, blue scrubs and white lab coats. The first tentative diagnosis (low ovarian reserve), the first treatment, Gonal and Ovitrelle, a follicle count and the final decisive move: artificial insemination.

The same pastel waiting room, again and again. Infrequently-updated magazines. Other couples on their own journeys in the seats next to them, now, suddenly, competitors: who will get there first, me, you, them? Who will never reach the finish line, elbow jabs, telepathic kicks, dirty play, in short, a free-for-all.

If you look at the advertising for fertility clinics, they are simply offering a service, meeting a demand, clean, scientific, efficient. You want something – a blonde baby – and, if you put yourself in their hands, then you will have one. The success rate is 90%, if you believe the ads. Nothing is impossible in this advanced phase of capitalism. Both spiritual and material needs are met, not to mention the need to reproduce, which falls into the grey area between the two.

You want it? You can have it! Though not without a fight, of course. Fists up or shut up. No one likes a whiner. No one. So suck it up.

Neoliberal language is truly emotive, inspiring, empowering, and corrupt. It turns desires into rights and rights into desires. Lie down here, spread your legs. Concentrate on your dreams, if you wish for them hard enough, they'll come true.

Dammit, you didn't wish hard enough! The first attempt fails. You've spent two weeks without making any sudden moves, going without ham, without beer, and guess what: here's your period! Repugnant, putrid blood. Failure, in other words.

Would you like to speak with our psychologist? He can see you on Monday. He can help you pick up the pieces of your shattered illusions and start the process all over again with new energy and a positive attitude. Did we mention our flexible payment plans? Besides, now you know what to expect. You're familiar with the pain – before insemination, you'll need to inject yourself in the belly every day, which will cause severe bruising again – all the unintelligible jargon is familiar to you now – recombinant gonadotropins, oestradiol levels, you've already learnt how to deal with guilt – it's my fault, I must be doing something wrong – if you know how to put the inevitable feeling of injustice to work for you – why me and not her, or her?

Then there are all the people around you. By now you know it's better not to tell them too much. Three kinds of birth control and they still get pregnant. Those people. The ones who tell you not to obsess about it, who say relax, enjoy, you just need a good lay, ha ha ha, it'll happen when you least expect it, like it happened to their co-worker's cousin.

People.

Don't talk to people.

Silence is better.

Your poor partner. How could you ever have imagined something like this? In the beginning, God created the heaven and the earth. God created man in his own image, male and female he created them. And God blessed them, and God said unto them, 'Be fruitful, and multiply, and replenish the earth, and subdue it.' He said nothing about artificial insemination, Gonal or Ovitrelle.

We mustn't think couples are always made stronger by situations like these. If the problem lies with the man – and it usually does – his masculinity may be wounded: low self-esteem, shame, violent reactions, none of these are rare. If the problem lies with the woman, it's common for her to expect the man to leave her; why would he stay with me when any other woman would be more fertile? It's not for nothing that in all misogynistic cultures – in all cultures – infertility has always been one of the most acceptable reasons for abandoning your wife. Or the most legitimate reason for taking a concubine. In fact, Jacob's wife Rachel, when she saw she couldn't have children, gave her handmaid Bilhah to Jacob so that she might bear him progeny. And so she did; he was no slouch, that Jacob.

And, as if this weren't enough, if state-of-the-art clinics have a 90% success rate, that means that one uterus in ten will never bear a child and give birth. And that risk is always present. It weighs heavily. It's a constant threat. But, don't give up, be strong, keep fighting! No one likes a loser, a whiner, a crybaby.

Sorry to bother you again, but did we mention our interest-free payment options?

As soon as I left the waiting room (to be honest, they showed me the door, once I told them what I wanted), I realised that my focus was all wrong. I wrote the lines above as if Alice/Jade were any woman with fertility problems, as if she were any ordinary woman with the sweet dream – occasionally the bitter nightmare – of holding her baby in her arms. And that, of course, is not what I should be doing. But I still don't know what I should do, other than to just keep on going. Which is why I'm in this clinic. Looking at these mothers- (and fathers)-to-be. Why I tried to speak with the doctors, reining in my shame. And finally, why the pudgy receptionist is the only person who takes pity on me, when she sees me sitting in the café with only my little notebook for company. She's a gossip, thank goodness. She remembers Alice, of course, her name is taboo at the clinic; no one wants to talk about her, but everyone remembers the couple's treatment. But even she can't tell me whether I should treat Alice like any other mother-to-be. They did, at least. Alice was a woman of extremes. She could be on top of the world, or down in the dumps. Never in between. That's all she could tell me.

In any case, after three cycles – three rounds of injections, ultrasounds, follicle counts – there was still no pregnancy, and the clinic recommended that they take the next step: in vitro fertilisation, life created in a test tube, and a much longer, more expensive, more painful and demoralising process than simple insemination.

They said yes, of course. They had long since passed the point of no return.

A WORKING HYPOTHESIS. PERHAPS SHE DIDN'T WANT CHILDREN. Perhaps that's why she didn't get pregnant naturally. Perhaps she was secretly taking the pill, secretly using a diaphragm, knew when her fertile days would be and slyly avoided sex, perhaps the desire not to be a mother was enough in itself to prevent fertilisation. Faith in the power of the mind again (don't obsess about it, just enjoy it, then when you least expect it ...). Perhaps she went to the first consultation thinking it would be the only one, that it would make her husband happy, and then for the next two years found herself down a rabbit-hole she couldn't get out of, who knows why? Perhaps she didn't do the Gonal shots correctly, perhaps she made the dose too small (I've seen the syringes, you have to turn the top to get the right amount, as prescribed by the doctor), perhaps when she was left alone after the insemination, she didn't even try for the recommended orgasm; instead placing her hands on her belly, praying for the sperm to go somewhere else.

Or maybe she did. Maybe Alice did everything that could be expected of a woman. Maybe, like Hannah in the Old

Testament, unable to bear children and in anguish, she made a promise to God: 'O Lord of hosts, if thou wilt indeed look on the affliction of thine handmaid, and remember me, and not forget thine handmaid, but wilt give unto thine handmaid a man child, then I will give him unto the Lord all the days of his life.' Yes, this is just as believable. Alice wanted her own blonde child in her arms and was willing to make any sacrifice right from the beginning.

And until the end.

I NEED TO EMPATHISE WITH THE CANDIDATES IN THE WAITING room. Their hopes and their frustrations. Empathise. Even though my own experience was very different. In my case, there was no primrose oil, no grapefruit juice, no folic acid, no basal temperature monitoring or holding my legs in the air after ejaculation. I got pregnant by accident. It's a little embarrassing for me to talk about this rookie error, the mistake of a witless teenager. I knew it could happen. I'm surrounded by unplanned pregnancies, to be honest, but I always wondered: when a stable couple in their thirties told me that it happened 'by accident,' I always wondered exactly how it could have happened. Was it truly unplanned, or did that mean 'without talking about it,' 'implicitly decided,' 'not explicitly stated,' 'letting nature do its thing without us actually agreeing to anything,' but taking all the necessary steps, following the biological mandate in a somewhat cowardly way, to its inevitable conclusion. Well, I was wrong. It is indeed possible for a stable, highly-educated adult couple to have an unplanned pregnancy. In our case, let's just say that, after a few years of trying the various annoying methods of contraception, we started using the one method that is never recommended. It worked reliably for about a year, but that turned out to be the calm before the storm.

When I was four days late, we went down to the pharmacy because we wanted to rule out the possibility of pregnancy as early as possible. When I saw the positive on the pregnancy test, it took two whole days before I started to believe it.

I wanted children, but in an abstract, general way. I told myself I still had four or five years. This was not the right time. In addition to finishing and publishing a novel, I had only just begun to enjoy its unexpected success. For reasons that would be obvious only to a skilled psychoanalyst, I had spent my entire youth turning my back on my vocation, and now, barely into my thirties, I had finally begun to find my place, a certain strength, and an unimaginable source of satisfaction in writing. From the discouraging feeling of being so near and yet so far – near enough to hear noises, laughter, sighs through the wall – I had gone to feeling that I now occupied my rightful place in the centre. And I was certain things would continue in the same way. More books, more readers, a whole life dedicated to a spectacular and more complete world that went far beyond all that. I don't mean vanity, prizes or praise. I mean what comes before – and after – all that: a new clarity, a private awareness that begins in the gut and then emanates from within, an instinctual feeling telling me that I could change the world for the better by filling a white screen with black scribbles. That's what I'm talking about. I had no need for babies in my new vision of the world.

And then there was Niclas. My friend, my lover, a fine and genuinely good man, reliable and well-mannered. A blonde and blue-eyed Swede, though not particularly handsome, even by our standards. Niclas. Was he the one who was destined to be the father of my children? I wasn't sure. Could I imagine him in the delivery room, whispering words of encouragement in my ear? No. To be honest, I couldn't even imagine myself in the delivery room. As I said, I had never put myself in the shoes of a woman whose waters had broken, whose cervix had dilated, a woman who had to push a child out of her vagina and into the world.

So, no. I had never imagined Niclas as a father.

Perhaps, as in the fantasies I shared with my high school friends, I might have seen myself as a single mother: my daughter and I, the two of us against the world, always victorious.

No. Not that either.

I've had two types of relationships in my life: ones that made me drunk with love, but made me suffer, and ones that were comfortable and pleasant, but lukewarm. I always thought that one day I would find a relationship that would bring together the best of both worlds: intoxication without suffering, comfort without apathy. But instead, I was with Niclas, the latest member of the second group. He was the one who was responsible for the growth and development of our relationship, always adapting to my wishes and desires. It seemed like the natural order of things: he gave, I received, and everyone was happy. He left his job in London as a well-paid and better exploited city worker when I decided to return to the Basque Country. With great effort, he has adapted to this bleak city of mine, to a miserable job and an even worse salary. But it's impossible to be grateful when someone gives you everything.

For a few weeks I thought the pregnancy was Niclas' fault, and resented him for it. Had he done something without my knowledge? Was that even biologically possible? Certainly, his desire to be a parent was much stronger than mine. He knew, for example, what a Maxi-Cosi was, what the term 'transitional objects' meant. These things interested him because they were part of his future. When he talked about children, it was never as a mere possibility; he spoke from a firm and fully realised perspective.

Despite my doubts and resentments, a couple of days after I found out I was pregnant, I felt an undeniable responsibility and I didn't care where that feeling came from; whether it was a biological imperative or something imposed on me by a patriarchal system, I accepted it, having given up on conspiracy theories, and began to truly want the baby. And I even learnt what a Maxi-Cosi is.

I learnt a lot of other things too. Lots of unpleasant words, for example: meconium, lanugo, amniocentesis, progesterone, vermix, prodromal labour, colostrum. I'm convinced that when women finally own our own pregnancy and labour once and for all, we'll have to set about rewriting the dictionary. It's not possible to feel like this journey is fully ours, to grasp the enormity of the changes, with this ugly lexical labyrinth that suggests a state of being somewhere between terminal illness and a Biblical curse. Perhaps we should take inspiration from nautical terminology: wake, anchor, shellfish, skiff. That's the way to go, dammit!

But I can't complain. I knew nothing about follicle counts, natural killer cells (which protect the mother but attack the fetus), anti-Müllerian hormone, heparin injections (to prevent miscarriage), and all those things women with fertility issues end up knowing by heart. I didn't even know they existed. I had seen pregnancy as a silent threat, a skilled sniper who would end the life I loved.

Perhaps Alice also saw it that way. And she was left fending for herself, at the mercy of that squadron of white lab coats at that elegant clinic, with no means of defending herself.

THE PREGNANCY WAS CONFIRMED WITH A BLOOD TEST. I CAN imagine the couple's cautious happiness. Ritxi would provide the happiness, and Alice the caution. Following the couple's instructions, they transferred two embryos into Alice. Another three were frozen for further attempts, or to donate later on. Given the quality of the embryos, they were told the probability of having twins was average. Ritxi was none too fond of the word 'average.' They were told about the risks of carrying twins: hypertension, early labour, caesarean. Even so, they wanted both: a pair of wild cards. A few days later, ultrasound revealed that both were indeed viable.

I remember my relief when my twelve-week ultrasound showed there was only one heartbeat. But Niclas' first words when we left the clinic were 'What a shame, only one!'

4
FORENSIC MEDICINE

O love, how did you get here?
O embryo
Remembering, even in sleep,
Your crossed position.
SYLVIA PLATH

THE WORD *ACT* IS USED IN CRIMINAL LAW TO TALK ABOUT THE events that led up to the trial, or rather, to avoid naming the events. As long as the events are still on trial, it's not permissible to define them more precisely. Until it's been proven, it didn't happen. The truth hides behind the word. I will also wear the mask of the word for the moment: *the act*. Killing, murder, homicide, assassination, double drowning, these words catch on my fingertips.

In any case, in November of the year of *the act*, I visited the house in Armentia for the first time. One of Niclas' co-workers covered his afternoon class, and our whole family went to Gasteiz to accept the Euskadi Award. My father would also come, on his own a little bit later; he had errands to run in Bilbo. My mother couldn't find any cheap plane tickets – it's difficult, apparently, in November. I told her not to worry about it, that it was just a formality and we'd celebrate the next time she visited.

The rain was chucking it down, we were having dreadful weather and yet, before the event, I convinced Niclas to go to the neighbourhood in Gasteiz with the highest per capita income. We had no trouble finding a parking space and, thanks to the photos shared by the press, I identified the house straight away. We found it just to the right of a field where an annual pilgrimage takes place, close to the Roman basilica and a reasonable distance from all the other villas. There it was, standing stolidly in the rain, as if nothing of note had ever happened inside. The whole façade of the second floor was made of glass, though it was now all covered with beige blinds. The rest of the house imitated the traditional structure of a Basque farmhouse, including exposed timber and a gabled roof. It was locked up tight, but someone was taking good care of the garden. I didn't know whether it was for sale, I imagined it was, but there was no sign on display. In Hong Kong, houses that have witnessed a suicide or some other crime are called *hongza*, or 红咋, and their market value is very low: an excellent opportunity for investors who believe in people's short memory spans. In Japan, these kinds of residences are called *Jiko Bukken*, or 事故物件, and there are websites where you can apply a filter to find such stigmatised houses. The grim details are shown next to the cheaper price: how many people died, how they died, when. ...

Two babies, drowned in the tub, in the middle of summer. *The act.*

Could you tell? Was there some sort of vibration in the air? A sombre atmosphere? I said yes, Niclas said no, it was just November and raining, that's all. The baby was asleep in his baby carrier and the three of us were getting wet under our single umbrella. And it would be dark soon besides. It was obvious Niclas wasn't comfortable standing in front of the house, but who would have been? What would the neighbourhood kids do when they had to pass by it? Would they bring their friends, tell them a story full of grisly details? Or was *the act* taboo in the neighbourhood, like it was at the clinic, a matter to be covered up and buried forever, everyone worried about the damage it might do to the reputation of that affluent hill and the market value of their own properties?

We saw no neighbours, so I couldn't ask.

Back in the car, I took a few notes about what we had seen on the way to the presidential offices, not noticing that my hair was plastered to my head by the rain. It's obvious in the photos from that day that I hadn't looked in a mirror before accepting the award from the President. People posted comments about it on Twitter. And they also said I had only received the award because I was a woman.

THE FIRST FEW DAYS ARE PRETTY STRAIGHTFORWARD. WELL documented. That's important in a judicial trial. When I'm trying to put together the whole story, I don't know to what extent it's helpful, or whether it actually puts me at a disadvantage.

There were never any other suspects. There was no indication of a third person, and the cameras outside the house recorded no one in the four hours between the nanny's departure and her return. No wolves, no dingoes. The possibility of an accident was also ruled out, as two identical accidents of that type are beyond all laws of probability. The press suggested that the first might have been involuntary manslaughter and that the mother, overwhelmed by what she'd done, in a state of total shock, her mind completely out of control, then committed the second murder. Pure speculation. From the point of view of the forensic police, at least, the case was simple, and all the evidence and reports were submitted to the court without delay.

After she killed her son and daughter, Alice was taken to Santiago Hospital, as a detainee at that point, where she was taken to the seventh floor, which normally houses alcoholics and anorexics. The psychiatrist on call confirmed that Alice was 'disoriented and in shock,' leaving room for a possible later diagnosis of dissociative amnesia in her records. They gave her sedatives. She barely spoke, but from time to time murmured *Where are they?* or *They're fine now, aren't they?* When they asked her name, she stated that her name was Jade, which confused the psychiatrists. A police officer guarded the door the whole time. The forensics team took her clothes, bagged them up and swabbed her hands for evidence. It was very late when, at last, they let her sleep. The forensic psychologists sent by the judge arrived the next morning, for three hours of tests in the same room, now with a new officer on guard. Alice refused her breakfast, but had begun to respond a little by then. She asked after her children and, when they told her what had happened, said it was impossible, that she would never do such a thing. She screamed, sobbed, then at last fell silent, only for the trembling to start again.

That morning a defence lawyer came to the hospital, a soft-spoken man who looked younger than his years. He had spent half the night at the police station, helping a boy who had – allegedly – assaulted a supermarket security guard, but now found himself in a totally new situation. He had worked as a defence lawyer for eight years, but he had never seen anything like this. It was difficult for him to get a handle on the situation, and the near-catatonic state of his client, the stifling heat, and the fact that he hadn't slept in twenty-six hours didn't help matters any. But in the end, he stepped up to the plate and, at the very last minute, advised his client to exercise her right not to testify before a judge. And the client heeded the words of the sweaty little man.

That afternoon, when the judge visited the hospital, he got nothing out of Alice but her last remaining sobs.

By then, the results of *the act*, the two small corpses, were in the Basque Institute of Legal Medicine on Gasteiz Avenue, awaiting autopsy. The autopsy brought no surprises, and no one had expected it to: death by drowning, the same cause of death in both cases. Foam in the lungs, water in their stomachs, the left ventricle of their hearts empty of blood. Those little hearts allowed for no other hypothesis.

The next day, the investigating judge issued an arrest warrant and Alice was taken to Zaballa Prison, with a prescription for sleeping pills and sedatives. It was not yet clear whether she was fully aware of what she had done. All sorts of opinions could be found in the press. One concerned citizen of Gasteiz declared that 'an eternity in hell wouldn't be enough to pay for what that evil woman did,' while another concerned citizen wrote, 'when she realises what she's done ... that will be a life sentence in itself, poor woman!'

Alice spent a total of five days in prison, all of them in the infirmary, since no one knew exactly what to do with her or what protocols to follow. Prisons weren't built with women like Alice in mind.

Ritxi did not go home after he left the police station. They say a co-worker picked him up in a car and took him back to their house in Eltziego for a few days. I read that in one newspaper, the rest of them said nothing about Ritxi at all. He is missing from all other accounts; how he spent those days will remain a mystery forever.

During the five days that Alice spent in jail, three key things happened. The first, though painful, was completely predictable, while the other two would have been difficult to predict. First, the twins were cremated in a funeral home in the suburbs of Gasteiz. Only Ritxi, his brother (who had just arrived from Austin), and a few close friends were present. They came and went by car. There are no photos from inside the funeral home. I don't know if any poems were read during the funeral, or any songs sung. It's better that way. What kind of person would want to know such details? Not even I.

Second, although the media had initially taken the opposite position for several days, they suddenly became sympathetic towards Alice. If you read through the archives with a certain level of detachment, as I'm doing now, the change is quite remarkable. They said she was broken, unable to accept what she had done, it would be punishment enough for her to live with what she did, she would never get over it, she would already be living in hell forever. Postpartum depression was mentioned for the first time, in a quote from a neighbour (I wrote their name down but could never find any trace of the person), and expert psychiatrists were interviewed. Perhaps they chose to reframe the events in order to stretch out their readers' curiosity for as long as possible? The motivations of the media are often pretty mundane. Who knows? In any case, public opinion lapped it all up and happily discarded the dark chronicle of the acts in favour of what was now a Greek tragedy.

And finally, in the most baffling act of all, Ritxi hired a really good defence lawyer for Alice. The day after the cremation, he broke his isolation in the Rioja Alavesa to speak with a lawyer he trusted, and ask for the name of the most experienced criminal defence lawyer in the city. One name came up immediately, a woman called Carmela Basaguren, who was close to retirement but was known for being a tough fighter and a feminist. She agreed to take the case that very day. Their first priority was now to get Alice out of Zaballa Prison. The appeal was sent immediately to the judge. All the reasons for ending Alice's incarceration were laid out in precise detail: it would be impossible for her to repeat the same crime, she had roots in the community, there was no flight risk, etc.

Furthermore, it was expected that the defence would argue in favour of an acquittal, citing temporary insanity as the reason for Alice's inability to be responsible for her actions. Yes, this was a possibility, as specifically stated in Article 20.1 of the Penal Code and, as Carmela Basaguren reminded the judge, punctuating her own eloquent statements by citing the Article word for word: *he shall be exempt from criminal liability who, at the time of committing the criminal offence, due to any anomaly or psychic alteration, cannot understand the illegality of the act or act in accordance with that understanding.*

The prosecution did not agree with the appeal, she was charged with two counts of first degree murder, the maximum charge times two, plus the circumstances of the family relationship, all of which could mean a maximum sentence of 40 years. But the judge, to the surprise of some, ruled in favour of the defence. Alice's passport was revoked, and she had to check in at the courthouse every two weeks and pay €50,000 in bail, but she was free.

The murderer was free. So was the ghost.

THERE IS A MYTH THAT HAS ITS ROOTS IN PRE-HISPANIC TIMES but flourished in the colonial era. The myth tells the story of La Llorona, a woman who killed herself, overcome by guilt after throwing her son and daughter (sometimes it was only one child, a son or daughter) into a river to drown. She is doomed to weep for all eternity, and to wander waterside areas forever. From Mexico to Chile, the story told is essentially the same and the same mythemes (interchangeable elements that make up the myth, similar to the pieces of different jigsaw puzzles) are repeated. In most versions, the children are drowned in a stream or lake, though in some cases, they are stabbed. In other retellings (in Panama, for example), the children die because of the mother's negligence; she goes dancing and leaves her children on the banks of the river. Often, she has been seduced, and then abandoned after the birth of the children. Alone and without resources, she sees no other way out and so decides to kill her children. Other times, she is utterly enraged, a Hispanic Medea, who aims to hurt the man that abandoned her by destroying the fruits of their bygone love.

In any case, the results are always the same: a wandering soul, eternal damnation, infinite tears adding water to water.

THAT NIGHT I DREAMT OF AUSTRALIA. ALTHOUGH I'VE NEVER paid any attention to my dreams before, I feel the need to mention this one. I didn't remember much the next day, a vague image of a dry Australian landscape, the sense of some undefined threat, nothing more. As the day wore on, the dream continued to haunt me, so I reviewed what I had written the day before. Four or five pages were all it took before I found this peculiar word: *dingo*. What exactly is a dingo? A wild dog, native to Southeast Asia, but very common in Australia. *Canis lupus dingo*. Why had I written about a dingo? The answer lies in a film I saw as a child, and I quickly found the connection by googling the word *dingo*.

17th August, 1980, somewhere near Mount Uluru (then known as Ayers Rock), in Australia's Northern Territory. In that ethereal landscape, the Chamberlain family are camping with their three children. They eat dinner around the barbecue, leaving the youngest child, 9-week-old Azaria, fast asleep in the tent. Midway through dinner, Lindy, the mother, hears what sounds like a dog barking. She's the only one of the family to hear it. She races for the tent and arrives, gasping for breath and expecting the worst, and indeed, she finds the worst: the tent is empty, there is no trace of the baby. Lindy has just enough time to spot the silhouette of a dingo disappearing into the darkness. She is the sole witness.

Little Azaria was never seen again.

The case could have been handled as an unfortunate accident, an urban myth to keep you awake at night, but it doesn't end there. After multiple twists and turns in the police investigation and a media trial, Lindy was sentenced to life in prison for the murder of her daughter. There was little evidence of *the act* – the body was never found, there was no motive, the alleged blood spattered on a pair of scissors turned out to be nothing but paint – but the mother's cold demeanour in front of the jury was a decisive factor in establishing her guilt and sentencing her to life imprisonment. Shortly after she went to prison, Lindy gave birth to a fourth child.

Lindy spent three years in prison, until new evidence came to light: shreds of Azaria's clothing were found in a dingo's den. As this evidence raised considerable doubt, she had to be released. Even so, the case was not officially closed until 2012, when it was duly noted on Azaria's death certificate that the killer was a dingo. Lindy received a hefty settlement from the Australian government for her unjust incarceration.

I don't know who let me watch the film, I think it must have been my father, since I used to spend weekends with him, watching television while he dozed beside me. I saw it all during those Saturday and Sunday afternoons, monsters aplenty to fuel my nightmares: Fu Manchu, killer sharks, plagues of ants, Marisol ... At the time, I didn't know that

Lindy Chamberlain's case was real, nor that it was (and still is) one of the most famous darker cases in Australia's legal history. However, it clearly left its mark on me as I can still remember it today, and since the word dingo, which sounds cheerful enough on its own, still haunts my dreams.

ULURU. DINGO. ULURU. DINGO.

Both are words that could be used in a title. Including the typographical quirk.

I'VE SEARCHED THROUGH NEWSPAPER ARCHIVES, LAWYERS' social media profiles, the penal code – both the current and previous versions – and forums where desperate citizens seek legal advice. I've devoted many hours to the task, and I don't think I've missed anything. The first few days are clear. Police procedures. The actions of the forensics team. The steps taken by the investigating judge. Even Ritxi's behaviour seems logical and easy to understand: fleeing the spotlight, seeking refuge with a friend, his state of shock, the denial and the other stages of grief that appear in textbooks.

But then things get confusing. I'm left in the dark, and no newspaper archive or official document can shed any light. I need to dig deeper. But which path do I take?

Something changed in Ritxi after he said his goodbyes to his children at the funeral service. This is the most striking about-turn. Alice's husband could have thrown in his lot with the prosecution and hired a lawyer (perhaps the same lawyer he chose for her defence – why not?) to ensure that she received the maximum possible sentence; after all, he was the third victim of the crime. But instead he decided to do everything he could to get his wife out of jail. Why? What textbook says that this might also be a stage of grief? Did he plan this from the beginning or did something make him change his mind? Was it love? Compassion? Denial? Complicity, even if only in a moral sense? And what did he have in mind for the future, if indeed he was looking to the future at all? Starting over, once his wife was free? A new life? A new city? Another IVF perhaps? Did it occur to him to think of the frozen embryos they still had? What did his friends say? His brother? Did anyone warn him to think things through, go slowly, take a step back?

When he picked Alice up at the prison gates, what were their first words to each other? You are forgiven, Alice. What I did cannot be forgiven, Ritxi. We can work it out, Alice. There's nothing to work out, Ritxi. I'll help you, Alice. I don't deserve your help, Ritxi.

A melodramatic conversation like this is the least likely scenario in such dramatic real-life circumstances.

How are you? Did they give you enough to eat? You look thinner.

Something along those lines seems much more probable.

In any case, they stayed together and left Gasteiz. They rented a small house in Eltziego, near Ritxi's work. Once every two weeks they went to the courthouse in Gasteiz, always together. The first time, two photographers were waiting for them. The next time there was no one at all. Once every two weeks they flew to Barcelona so Alice could see a famous psychiatrist. She started treatment for psychosis. She kept all the pills she had to take in a plastic case, the kind that's divided into separate compartments by day and time. And she started painting again, as part of her occupational therapy.

There are not many photos of Alice from this period. The media was starting to forget about her. Everyone had forgotten about her. The twins were ashes, and so was the marriage.

I IMAGINE THERE MUST HAVE BEEN GOOD TIMES. FALLING IN love, starting to plan a future with another person, skin to skin, breath to breath, understanding each other, building a shared routine, not understanding each other but still sharing an intimacy that would be incomprehensible to an outsider, built on words, hair, loving touches.

When Ritxi met Jade, she was already calling herself Alice. She was working as a model/actress in a corporate video for a famous Bordeaux winery. Ritxi was there by chance, on a free trip organised by an association for the advancement of viticulture. I can imagine the sudden jolt, not a painful one, that might be called falling in love. Alice's beauty and the scent of Ritxi's power, a gentle power, magnanimous, his expensive tie and well-groomed hair. He still looked young though he was ten years older than she was. He spoke French perfectly, and it was obvious that the world was his oyster. What more could Alice ask for? Same old story, nothing mysterious at all.

Ritxi asked if she was free for dinner. Alice said she was, with a smile that was half shy, half sly. Filming was over for the day and Alice was supposed to return to Avignon on the afternoon train, but there was a strike, so she had to spend another night. A lucky strike. They had dinner in an intimate place, a delightful bistro that Ritxi knew well. He chose the wine (one made by the competition, of course), a 2001 Château Latour-Martillac, not the most expensive on the menu, he didn't feel the need to show off. Alice did not know how rich Ritxi was yet, though she was trying to figure it out. She hardly tasted the wine. Ritxi told her about how, after studying in Paris and Washington, he had started working in his father's business, the family winery, and that it had been a year since his father had suddenly died, leaving him in charge of the business. He had a brother, a scientist who had no interest in the business. The winery had been owned by the family since it opened, and Ritxi taking over marked its fifth generation in the family. Alice was satisfied. He didn't tell her about his decision to expand his father's business, about his investments in wind power and boutique hotels. She would find all that out later. Alice felt increasingly comfortable talking to him, more and more at ease. She told him she was a vegetarian (Ritxi had noticed right away that she ate very little, pushing her food around on the plate), that she dreamt of being a painter but in the meantime made her living as a model here and there. She hated Avignon, she told him, especially in the summer. The heat. The mosquitos. She said nothing at all about her family and seemed to have an air of melancholy. She was all alone in the world. Ritxi found it all quite captivating.

He took her back to her hotel, a cheap little place on Rue Bouffard. Alice was sharing a room with a co-worker from the agency, another model/actress. They kissed, after Ritxi announced his intention – *I'm going to kiss you, Alice* – but he didn't go so far as to invite her back to his own elegant hotel room and Alice didn't ask, though she did imagine the freshly ironed sheets and fragrant bath salts. It was 2006, the world was all well connected by then and after all, they didn't live that far from each other, just a border away. Both of them were certain they would see each other again.

I read about all of this in an interview Ritxi gave five years ago, on a well-known website devoted to wine, in which he spoke openly about this romantic moment in his life. 'I Fell in Love With My Wife Over a Bottle of the Competition's Wine,' was the title of the interview, and it genuinely felt like the words of a man in love. Ritxi let down his guard in the interview, which was uncharacteristic for him.

Ritxi seems like a conventional upper middle class man who likes to think of himself as unconventional, based on the little I know about him. Instead of playing golf, he prefers riding his mountain bike. Instead of spending his holiday in an over-water hotel in the Maldives, he took the Trans-Siberian Express in total solitude, with just a backpack for company. He does yoga every morning and has a tarantula for a pet, in a glass terrarium – or had, until he got married. He's a fan of 1970s hard rock, especially Led Zeppelin. He always feels a bit out of place in meetings, just a little, a vague unease which he endures by gazing out the window or drawing intricate abstract figures in his notebook. He could see himself taking early retirement and doing some volunteer work: teaching immigrant children perhaps, or cleaning forests or beaches.

From the little I know of the world of advertising, executives like Ritxi are quite common. Moderate extravagance is an integral part of the curriculum vitae. In a traditional industry like the wine trade, however, I can easily imagine all the rumours and gossip there would have been about Ritxi.

That's why he chose Alice. Because he found her unconventional: her dark side, her aura of loneliness, her broken wings, her artistic talent that had never been fully realised and that triggered outbursts of frustration and rage. By then most of the men in his circle were married, not to mention the women, but he saw little variety in their spouses. The same Master's degrees, similar holidays, scant topics for conversation.

Alice wasn't like that. She was bright, and eager to adapt to any situation. He knew his choice would only increase the rumours and gossip, and that was fine with him. On the very day they met, he decided he would marry her. He imagined thunderstorms circling her, reconciliations, all the different colours of a dazzling spectrum enriching his life, a blazing happiness incomprehensible to others; envy, admiration, ignorance.

It was a game to him: the foreign greed of a selfish man accustomed to having it all.

Hence his responsibility.

Perhaps.

5
FAMILY FRIENDLY

*There is no more sombre enemy of good art than
the pram in the hall.*
CYRIL CONNOLLY

MUCH IS SAID ABOUT THE EXHAUSTION OF MOTHERHOOD, THE
lack of sleep, the bags under the eyes. But I think too little
is said about the hours of boredom. About the endless,
amorphous, indistinguishable days reduced to a grey routine
of breastfeeding, changing nappies, getting a crying baby to
sleep then checking to make sure he's still breathing. Isolated,
confined, working 24 hours a day at a job with all the social
status of a toilet cleaner (as I know all too well, having
worked cleaning toilets at one point), blank hours, a gaze
lost in the distance. Every moment of your life devoted to
the life of another. In a hypocritical society, which tells you
that a life devoted to another is a beautiful and even desirable
thing; a revolution, of sorts, a silent revolt in our society,
which moves according to a cost-benefit paradigm.

Yeah, right.

If it were such a beautiful, desirable, revolutionary thing,
men would have taken it over for themselves by now without
a doubt, sending women to work outside the home.

Anyway. ...

You can complain about exhaustion, but you can't complain about boredom. It's a frivolous complaint, unfathomable. If you're so bored, maybe you should have another child, or another seven like your grandmothers did. You think they had time to get bored? Puh-lease.

If the weather is nice, you can go out for a walk, and you can push the pushchair mile after mile, just to make sure you're the master of the rhythm of your own feet. If you stop in front of a shop window, seeking your own fading reflection, then the baby cries, reminding you to start walking again. On rainy days it's worse. Of course, your only option then is to look out of the window just to make sure the world is still there. The traffic lights, green, red, green, umbrellas bumping into each other, a plastic bag tearing, spilling a parade of oranges down the middle of the pavement. On days like these, a call from a telemarketer – provided it doesn't wake the baby – becomes a memorable event, a novelty, and you respond eagerly to the man with the lovely accent who lists all the advantages of switching to Jazztel. You begin to use the telemarketer's name as if you were friends: *really, Julio, how interesting, Julio, I'll have to think about it, could you call me back tomorrow?*

Doris Lessing wrote about it: 'there is nothing more boring for an intelligent woman than to spend endless amounts of time with small children'. I like this quote because it confirms that I am an intelligent woman. Elsewhere, Doris described motherhood as the *Himalayas of tedium*. In Rhodesia, pregnant at nineteen. And pregnant again at twenty. Lessing's legend is inextricably linked to her motherhood, because she abandoned the son and daughter (John and Jean) she had with her first husband, in Africa, in the area then known as Rhodesia (or, more specifically, Southern Rhodesia), to run off to London with her son from her second marriage, after her second divorce. That third child, Peter, died aged 66, and was cared for by Doris until his last breath – he was sickly his whole life. A few weeks after Peter died, the Nobel Prize-winning writer followed, at 94 years of age. A life devoted to another, until she was 94.

But let us speak plainly.

Sometimes it is a beautiful, desirable, revolutionary thing. Atop an eight-thousand-metre peak in the Himalayas of tedium, when you're exhausted and can't breathe, a spark ignites in a disconcerting and elusive moment that shakes you out of your routine and has an impact on you forever.

For example: you have the baby at your breast, as always, skin to skin, warmth to warmth, and suddenly you realise that his strong sucking doesn't hurt your nipples anymore, you even feel a sort of pleasure while he sucks, and the baby is focused and you are focused, enjoying the release of prolactin, relaxing into it. You could easily fall asleep, the world is dissolving, you and the baby are dissolving, you are one now, and then the baby pulls away, milk dripping from one corner of his mouth, and he looks right into your eyes and not only that, but he *sees* you, and he smiles and you smile back at him, a reciprocal smile of pure gratitude and love, and at that moment you know that you have reached the highest level of intimacy, that nothing can compete with this moment: the sensation in your nipples, the skin, the flow of warm milk, that smile, the most candid gaze.

I feel sorry for Niclas in those moments, genuine pity, because it occurs to me that he will never experience anything like this.

ANOTHER WRITER. ANOTHER MOTHER. THE SCOTTISH NOVELIST Muriel Spark. She also abandoned her son, in Rhodesia of all places, Southern Rhodesia. What is it about Southern Rhodesia? Little Samuel Robin, left in the care of his manic-depressive father in Zimbabwe, then known as Southern Rhodesia.

What if I call my book Rhodesia?

Uluru.

Dingo.

Rhodesia.

The list is getting longer.

WITH THE HELP OF THE NURSERY, THINGS CHANGED, OF course. The pangs of guilt I felt when I dropped Erik off disappeared as soon as I turned on my laptop and heard Windows launching. So much so that the four hours he spent there started to fly by. To save the time I would usually spend going home and coming back, I hung out in cafés near the nursery. I tried not to go to the same places too regularly, since some of the café workers didn't appreciate me spending an entire morning over a single coffee.

And I wrote, I wrote with my whole body and soul, I wrote with the passion I had felt long ago. I was building Alice, little by little, whilst rebuilding myself.

Unfortunately, the creative euphoria of the early days quickly waned. For one thing, I was tired, since Erik was still breastfeeding three or four times a night. For another ... I don't know. I let the hours pass me by, spending my mornings reading the paper or searching the web for things unrelated to the documentation I needed. Some days I didn't write a single word. Other days I wrote very little, and the next day did nothing but delete what little I had written the day before. I was still called upon frequently to give talks, appear at book clubs, judge literary competitions; but I almost always had to say no, and found myself giving too many explanations: I had a small child to look after, his father was at work every afternoon, my parents didn't help at all ... I was frustrated when I went to the nursery to pick Erik up, and more frustrated to think about the long hours that lay ahead of me, suffering in advance: make lunch, feed Erik, try to get him to nap, have lunch with Niclas ... and by the time we put things away and Niclas went back to the academy, the baby had woken up again, sometimes while I still had my toothbrush in my mouth. There went my sweet plan to steal a five-minute nap on the sofa. We went out for a walk, weather permitting, and I would feed him a snack on the bench by a stream. Otherwise, we would lie on a blanket on the living room floor, me trying to read, Erik constantly expanding the limits of his mobility. He had started crawling, opening boxes, inspecting electrical outlets; he needed constant supervision. Goodbye, books. There was no way to read. Have a quick feed and let's see if it stops raining for once.

What would happen if I spent my afternoons writing? I wondered. How different would the results be? I imagined the afternoons would be much more productive, no way would I suffer the same creative drought as I did in the mornings, no, no, no, in the afternoons, oh the afternoons, the words, the sentences would flow, the story would advance on its own with unparalleled rhythm and originality, the knot in my head untangling at last. Then, at dusk, I would get in the car and go to Igorre, Durango or Agurain to be welcomed sweetly by a book club, where I would speak with ease about my book – about myself – in love with my words, my work, and my life in general. When the meeting was over, I would still have time for a glass of wine and a nibble with my readers – high school teachers, active retirees, warm, earnest women – and I would keep talking about my next project, and about the exotic journey I would have to make to finish my research, and everyone would admire me, praising my youth, my talent, even my beauty, to the skies, and when I took out my wallet to pay for the drinks, everyone would say, no, please, forget about paying, c'mon, it's on us, it will be an honour, and I would go back home exhausted but happy, with the satisfaction that only a writer can feel at the end of a glorious working day.

But, instead of all that, I had to change nappies, wash one load of laundry after another, take out a tit whenever the baby wanted, entertain the baby, who now needed constant entertainment.

I thought about leaving him at the nursery a few hours longer, very tempting, but I didn't know how I would justify it to Niclas, to the nursery practitioners; I don't know why it was so important to me to look like a good mother to those kind workers, or to myself. Especially to myself.

When I went to the nursery at midday, Erik would immediately notice my presence and, no matter what he was doing, he would drop everything, crawl over to me on all fours and reach his sweet arms up to me from the ground, suddenly impatient, his little face all lit up. *Mama! You came for me again, you didn't forget me today either, you have no idea how grateful I am, Mama.* He would hug me, and I would tell myself I should be enjoying these moments. I would never love another body the way I loved that body, his perfect spine, his cheeks, his soft little bottom, his exquisite skin that I covered with kisses. After all, that was also life, that was especially life, that unique energy and brilliance. I would have to be an idiot not to relish it to the full. But something was escaping me. Something wasn't working right inside me. If I could just soak it all in, that energy and brilliance would surely show itself in my writing, this profound knowledge of life would have to come out in my writing sooner or later.

Wouldn't it?

I wasn't so sure.

IT WAS NEARLY SUMMER, AND THAT GAVE ME AN OPPORTUNITY. We had agreed not to go on holiday, we had to save, to make the prize money last as long as possible, and a two-week visit from Niclas' parents was the only break in routine that we could hope for.

But I had to see Léa. It was becoming clearer and clearer to me that, if I was going to move forward with my writing, I would need to talk it over with my friend, who had known the young Jade well. In our occasional texts, Léa had remained as close-mouthed as she had been when I first raised the topic. I had told her, out of sheer anxiety, that I had started writing about the case, but I told her it was an assignment; that it had started as a newspaper report, and now they wanted me to make it into a whole book. I often make up crazy little lies like this. They're absurd lies that don't change anything and are undoubtedly aimed at myself. For example, the absolute height of absurdity: once, in a taxi, the metre said €8.76 and I gave the driver a ten-euro note, telling him to take nine, and made up an explanation. I needed the euro in change for my daughter, who had just lost a tooth, so I could leave it under her pillow. I had no daughter, of course. I just didn't want to give the driver the whole note but, at the same time, didn't want to appear a cheapskate. In the end, all I managed to accomplish was to feel like an idiot. In this case, I think I said it so that Léa wouldn't think I was being morbid, so I could convince the both of us that there was a deep, professional, and therefore acceptable interest behind my obsession. She responded brusquely to my messages, but I was sure that, if we could see each other in person, her attitude would change and we would develop a real understanding, an honest and enlightening conversation.

I found a solution. Instead of writing, I spent a few days looking at hotel ads, starting at the Côte d'Azur (too expensive) and ending on the coast of Girona. I finally found a surprisingly cheap hotel, with half board, in Roses, rather far away from the beach. Most of the reviews on Tripadvisor were bad – old mattresses, too noisy, greasy buffet … – but we couldn't afford anything better, and the hotel was supposed to be 'family friendly', which I thought was worth taking into account. The cost put me in a bit of a tight spot, to be honest. Every extra expense would mean less time that I had to write, and the earlier I would have to return to work. But on the other hand, the book screamed out for the journey.

When I presented my plan to Niclas, I didn't tell him about my true purpose. At first, I only explained the benefits for Erik of a week in the Mediterranean, then the few small pleasures it would mean for us – paella, Empordà wine, the warm sea. I mentioned the chance to visit Léa later, after we had already made the reservations, as if it had only just occurred to me. This conversation with Léa was essential if the book were to progress. It was a four-hour trip; I would spend one night in Avignon, and the baby was nearly a year old by now, so had to start getting used to the breast not always being available. I would never have suggested such a thing if it weren't truly essential for the book.

As with all negotiations, I had to sacrifice something in return. I agreed that Niclas could go to the mountains one weekend in September and stay overnight. No problem. No problem at all.

SO WE SET OFF ON THE EVE OF SAINT IGNATIUS DAY, ALL THREE of us in the car. Little Erik coped with the journey remarkably well. He slept in the car better than he ever did at home. I had a nap too, as we crossed the parched lands of Aragon. It was a lovely moment, thanks to the air-con.

All our grim suspicions about the hotel were about to come true, however. It was old and full of kids. A meeting place for every large family in Eastern Europe, apparently. While the parents lounged on deck chairs and chain smoked, margaritas in hand (getting as much out of their 'all inclusive' wristbands as they possibly could), the hotel took charge of the swarms of children: a water polo match in the swimming pool, archery and ping-pong tournaments on the lawn, fancy dress parties, recycled arts and crafts, a kitsch 'mini disco' at night. From time to time, we saw childless couples or people on their own, and I couldn't understand who had tricked them into going there, and why they didn't run away screaming in terror, forever traumatised.

Erik was too little to hand over to the underpaid hotel staff in orange t-shirts, so we left early in the morning and didn't return to the miserable hotel until dinnertime. The plan was to spend the day at the beach, but we soon realised that this was not the best idea for a small child with extremely fair skin. We couldn't go to the most beautiful coves without packing a full load: toys, beach umbrella, thermos flasks, bottles, sun creams in a variety of SPFs, it was all far too complicated. But, if we tried to get settled on the more crowded beaches, Erik just ate sand and cried when we put him in the water, terrified by the gentle waves of the Mediterranean. He clawed the hat off his head and refused to stay in the shade, wriggling over the sand like a lizard to find his next mouthful. We lasted for around forty minutes of sheer frustration on the beach, then decided on 'cultural tourism' instead: we visited Cadaqués, Figueres and the capital city of Girona, perpetually in search of shade. We all slept badly at night, and the air-con was no help whatsoever: our only options were infernal noise or stifling heat.

On the fourth day, after filling Erik's tummy with my milk and giving him a few quick cuddles while pulling a sad face, I set off. I left, and I truly believe I have never had a deeper feeling of freedom than when I headed for France that day on the N-II for Perpignan/Peralada/La Jonquera, just barely managing to stick to the speed limit.

I SEE LÉA ONCE EVERY TWO OR THREE YEARS, SO MAYBE FIVE times or so at the most since our uni days. We've made plans to meet in London, Paris or Avignon, though only for quick holidays or weekends. That's been it, since we met. However, the distance between us never grows; we always greet each other as if we'd been together just the night before, picking the conversation up exactly where we left off. We have a shared past – intense, if brief – and it serves us well. Ours is a friendship that will never be tainted; it is handled with care and idealised by the simple fact that we so rarely see each other. We would forgive each other anything.

Even though they had just moved to a town outside Avignon, we planned to meet in the city centre, in the square in front of the papal palace, at 8 p.m. I had to wait twenty minutes for her to arrive, and the heat was unbearable, much worse than on the coast. I drank the first beer I ordered in one gulp and debated whether to order a second. Since I wasn't going to feed Erik for several hours, I didn't have to worry about getting drunk. For the first time in nearly two years.

Every single year, I've always felt a sort of divine signal that summer has arrived, and it always puts me in a good mood immediately. Sometimes the signal comes to me well before summer: on the first warm day in May, for example. It might be something specific, like lying in the grass on a starry night, a faint scent of verbena, the first sip of a mojito with lots of mint. Other times, it's nothing I can put my finger on specifically, just an abstract feeling, something in the air, the indefinable scent of some invisible ether perhaps, an undercurrent of excitement in those around me. I got the signal that year while I was sitting in that outdoor café, in front of the papal palace, with my second beer. It's summer. I'm summer. It was August by then, but better late than never, as they say.

It was the second time I'd been to Avignon. I had visited seven years ago, for the civil baptism of Léa's first child, and everything was as I remembered, more or less. They hadn't baptised their next two children – girls, who would have been four and two that summer, I thought – unsurprisingly, since the first baptism and the party after it had been rather unfortunate.

But I'll get to that later, because Léa is here at last, now that I'm halfway through my second beer, and we have loads to talk about.

IT WAS A MAN FROM GASCONY CALLED BERTRAND DE GOT, BETTER known to history as Clement V, who was the first pope to establish his official residence in Avignon. Though initially only temporary, in the end seven popes lived and found refuge here throughout most of the 14th century, far away from Rome and all its conspiracies. The palace is one of the largest Gothic buildings in the world; the walls are said to be five metres thick, but the last time I was here, I managed to get in for free by sneaking through the door of the gift shop when the security guard wasn't looking. I ran through the stone halls thinking I'd get caught and be thrown out, but nothing happened.

I no longer engage in furtive tourism, however. This time I've come specifically to talk to Léa.

Here we are, my friend and I, on a hot summer night. Flowered dresses, sandals, tattoos visible on each of us, mine on my ankle, hers on her shoulder blade. A couple of beers in front of us. Chatter and giggles.

We are young again.

So much so that, caught up in the energy of friendship, I completely forget about Jade/Alice. We talk about ourselves, comfortable in our own skin and with each other. Memories of the past, plans for the future, rumours and gossip. I don't have to watch the clock or breastfeed anyone. And, not only do I not have to do it, I don't even have to think about not having to do it. But finally, I can feel that my breasts are too full, and I have to go to the toilet to release some of the pressure of the milk into the basin, to literally milk myself, and when I get back, we inevitably talk about children. Most of our old friends from Apartments A and B have stumbled into parenthood, but Léa was the pioneer: she was only 23 when Matthias was born. For some people, the natural result of falling in love is an uncontrollable desire to reproduce and, though I was surprised when she told me she was pregnant, I had always thought she would be one of those people.

'Are you sure you want to stay in the hotel? You know we have plenty of room at the new house.'

'Yes, I'm sure. Nothing personal. I'd just like to spend one night alone, just one.'

'Okay, but don't think I'm going to let you leave early tonight!'

'No, of course not. Another beer then? And how about something to eat?'

She didn't take it personally, of course, because she understands and probably approves, and might even envy me a little, since she has three kids of her own at home.

I had booked a room in a hotel I knew, the small Hôtel Médiéval, on a narrow street inside the city walls, where I had stayed seven years before, when I first came to the city for the baptism. I had come alone then, as well. I was dating a Colombian guy that I had met in London, and he had made it crystal clear that he had no intention of attending any tacky little social event in France with me. We split up soon after, which was predictable, and then Niclas came into my life. In the meantime, however, there was that short holiday that took me to Avignon for the civil baptism.

'The hotel is nice, the best rooms look onto the square,' Léa told me that first time, as she drove me there with little Matthias strapped into the car seat.

There may be legitimate reasons for being familiar with hotel rooms in your own city (refinishing the floors in your house, change of routine, who knows?), but the look she gave me told me that her reason was none too legitimate, or at least that's what she wanted me to think. I didn't want to continue the conversation. I went out onto the balcony overlooking the square.

'The hand soap is wonderful, mint, from Marseilles,' she added, going into the bathroom to see if this information was still correct.

That's when my suspicions began to grow, but instead of asking her anything, I opened up my suitcase on the bed, feeling uneasy. I'm generally discreet, and I often go shy.

'Shit, my dress for the baptism is all wrinkled,' I said, truthfully, but glad I had found something to say.

'Say it isn't so! Let me make a couple of calls, we'll have to call the whole thing off.'

In the end, I smoothed out my dress with my hands, and looked presentable enough at the service. It took place in the town hall, where the mayor wore a tricolour sash and I barely understood a single word or speech. The whole time, I was wondering whether this type of event, which dated from the Revolution – a civil baptism? really? – was meant to be taken ironically or not. The beautiful blonde baby was all smiles as he was passed from person to person. The dinner after the baptism was held at a hotel in the suburbs, next to a golf course. There was a beautiful garden, with a pond and everything. The food was delicious, the setting couldn't have been lovelier, and the heat was still bearable. I felt farther and farther away from the Colombian and, with all the champagne, I was sure I understood French much better, and was confident that if I played my cards right, I would be approached by some man I could take back to the Hôtel Médiéval. However, there was something sour in the air, which at first I put down to the less-than-festive French culture. Léa's husband, Albert, was drinking a lot, and Léa complained about how much the party was costing them every time she spoke to me, repeating again and again that it had been Albert's stupid idea.

Close to midnight, Matthias' grandmother took him off to bed and the rest of the grown-ups continued binge-drinking, all inhibitions lost. I felt as if I were lost, lost but happy, trying to communicate with strangers in a whirlwind of language and practically assaulting the waiters handing out drinks, all the while thinking myself quite charming, *sympa, très sympa*. The climax of the evening came soon afterwards, during the half-hearted dancing by the pond, when Albert dropped to his knees, clutching Léa's waist. At first, I took it for a drunken declaration of love, but I quickly saw he was crying like a baby. The DJ either didn't notice, or was a true professional (perhaps such *hyper bizarre* scenes were a daily occurrence for him?); either way, the music kept on playing and some of the guests kept on dancing and laughing, as if everything were normal. But I saw everything, and when Léa fled, leaving Albert on his knees, I went after her, completely forgetting my hesitation that afternoon.

I found her in the toilet, splashing water on her face.

'I'll take you back to the hotel, okay?'

I said yes and, alcohol notwithstanding, we made it back to the hotel safely, leaving the car in a car park. We didn't speak at all on the way back. Since the baby was with his grandmother, Léa didn't want to go home, so I said she could stay with me. On the bed, there at the Hôtel Médiéval, she gave me the lowdown.

It was a simple story. When she was three months pregnant, she met Fabrice, one of the dads at the school where she was doing her student teaching. It was like a lightning bolt that sparked a wildfire: totally beyond their control. They stayed at the Hôtel Médiéval four, five, six times, while Léa's pregnancy became more and more obvious. But the man (married, with two kids, twelve years older than she was) didn't seem to mind. He seemed willing to play father to the baby on the way. This was how Léa spent the sweet interlude of her pregnancy: caught up in a whirlwind of double adultery. It was addictive, a potent cocktail of anxiety, guilt and orgasms. There were many comings and goings, doubts, tears, melodramatic gestures; they broke up forever every two weeks. My friend didn't tell me everything, but I could imagine the rest: Léa was unsure, Fabrice backed off out of pride, then came harsh words, spite, scorn, a couple of days without calling each other, but they would always end up back at the Hôtel Médiéval. A month before she gave birth, Léa cut off all contact, suddenly feeling that she ought to act sensibly, but the evening after Matthias was born, she texted Fabrice from the hospital. Then, when the baby was just getting used to his life and home, Albert found out and the drama really began. Fabrice's wife found out too, and then everyone at the school knew. It seemed that everyone in the entire department of Vaucluse between the ages of 8 and 88 knew the whole story.

I had to get up from the bed at that point – the room was spinning – and vomited in the toilet with loud noises and no dignity. When I returned, Léa seemed calm, not drunk at all. She went on as if nothing had happened, while I curled up into a ball with my head beneath a pillow.

'A lover while pregnant, I broke a big taboo there, didn't I? Maybe a mother's biggest taboo.'

It was true that the story significantly affected me at the time, but I was only twenty-four and my own love life couldn't have been more ordinary. How rattled we are by our friends' stories may be a good measure of our own maturity. Fewer and fewer things surprise me these days. It's a feeling that fills me with despair, because I feel at times that I'm draining my glass of innocence, as the poet would say. Now, for example, I would never say that taking a lover while pregnant is the biggest taboo.

Not even close.

A BRIEF ASIDE, SO IT'S CLEAR ONCE AND FOR ALL WHAT A CULTURED person I am. Chastity, in Roman times, meant preserving the caste. A pregnant woman could go to bed with whomever she wanted because the lineage was ensured at that point. *I never take on a passenger, unless the ship is full*, in the words of Julia, daughter of the emperor Augustus, explaining how she remained chaste. Perhaps our way of understanding chastity is the strangest, since it has more to do with pleasure than with caste. Our chastity means the suppression of pleasure.

THEY BROUGHT OUT A DOZEN OYSTERS FOR US, AND TWO glasses of white wine. I don't like oysters, but find it impossible to say no if someone suggests them. I don't want to spoil the mood, and I do understand the aesthetic value of oysters. Any attempt at sophistication is doomed to failure if you say you don't like oysters. Besides, after abstaining for so long, the two cold beers (or was this the third?) had easily carried me into the euphoric phase of drunkenness, and I felt sure I had the courage to put a sticky amorphous mollusk in my mouth. Why not? *Allons, enfants de la Patrie!* It still didn't seem like the right time to talk about Jade though. The summer, the wine, my old friend and the oysters. Why talk about the madwoman who killed her babies? Why not forget that such things even happen? Fortunately, Léa remembered the main purpose of our meeting. As we ate the oysters, she remembered that the madwoman had taught her how to stick her fingers down her throat, and proceeded to give me the fifteen-minute version of two childhoods, two girlhoods.

THEY HAD ALWAYS HUNG OUT TOGETHER, EVER SINCE THEY met aged six. Jade was mischievous, scatterbrained, rather sly, and always brave. But she knew how to play whatever role the situation required. Léa often paid the price for her friend's antics. Jade was not a good student and didn't try to be; she didn't like reading and had no head for numbers. They both took the bus to school, but Jade always arrived at the bus stop alone, and always went home alone later. She lived with her mother and a younger half-brother. Jade often went to Léa's house, but Léa almost never went to Jade's. Her mother didn't work. She was half-deaf and, with two kids, received enough financial support to get by. She was skin and bones. She smoked a lot, and drank a lot too, probably. She kept a bottle of Listerine by the kitchen sink, and would gargle there quite often, spitting it out onto the dirty plates. Léa thought that was disgusting. There was no father. Once, Jade said he was a handball player who had fled Poland, but by the time she was born, he'd fled France too, always on the run. He had met her mother when she was working at a hotel. She gave him breakfast and he gave her a baby. There was no way of knowing whether this was true or pure fantasy. Jade probably didn't know either. There was a Slavic touch to her face though, those cat eyes, her cheekbones.

[First oyster.]

Once, after eating lunch in the school canteen, she took Léa into the toilets and showed her how to bring her food up by sticking her index and middle fingers down her throat. They both adopted the habit, and did it every day after lunch. Models did it too, it was a way of cleansing their insides. Léa liked it and started doing it after dinner too, at home. Her parents found out and took her to a psychologist. Jade and Léa were eleven years old and it was the first time they had been separated. Léa's parents said Jade was a bad influence. It wasn't a good time. Best not to talk about it any further.

[Second oyster.]

When the time came for them to go to secondary school, they were reunited. By then, Jade had started painting, and her talent was highly praised by her teachers. Léa played the piano, but to considerably less praise. From time to time, without saying anything to her friend, Léa would still go to the toilet to vomit. But not too often. She didn't want to set off any alarm bells. Léa had no way of knowing if Jade was still doing the same thing, although she liked to think so; she liked to think that their puking brought them together on a level so deep that no one else could reach it. Jade then joined a fine arts course, so they now went to different high schools. They saw each other downtown, went shopping, did a little shoplifting here and there, spent hours and hours by the river, making plans and drinking gin. Jade was always surrounded by boys, but shooed them all away to be with Léa. This made my friend very happy and filled her with pride.

Léa caught Jade telling little lies every now and then. She tried not to make a big deal of it. Mostly, it was because she was ashamed of her family, her mother was a wreck, her half-brother half retarded. Jade wanted to go to the Paris School of Fine Arts, the best art college in the country. Delacroix had gone there, Monet and Renoir. She had to prepare a proper portfolio. Léa helped her choose her best drawings and watercolours. She genuinely liked Jade's watercolours of women's bodies, they were like snakes. They were both excited about the Paris adventure, even though Léa had already agreed with her parents that she would study history at Avignon University. It was difficult to get accepted into the art college but Jade was good, she had brought her grades up quite a bit at school, and all her teachers were delighted with her watercolours: the snake women, again and again. One day in May, at 11 p.m., Léa had a telephone call that startled the whole family: it was Jade, calling her friend after spending the whole day on cloud nine. She had received a letter from Paris that morning: they had accepted her portfolio and were inviting her to take the practical exam. She couldn't believe it. She was afraid she would wake up from the dream. But Léa believed it; she had every confidence in her friend.

The day of the entrance exam was coming up fast, but there was more drama: Jade didn't have the money for the trip. Her mother didn't want to give her any and, since it was May, what little she had saved from her summer job (they had both worked in the same souvenir shop) was long gone. Jade managed to find money for the train fare and the hotel, taking some from her savings and some from her mother's wallet. For several days, Léa heard nothing from her friend, but she had high hopes for her passing the exam. In her mind, the plan was clear: starting next year, she would visit Jade in Paris, she would have an artist friend in the city who would discover bohemian spots and introduce her to interesting people. She saw it all so clearly that she was hardly surprised at all when Jade told her she had been accepted. They went out to celebrate. Tequila shots, one after another, all paid for by Léa. And a stern scolding from her parents when she got home drunk at four in the morning.

Then, in the summer, there was even more drama: after doing the calculations, Jade realised that, even with a scholarship, living in Paris was going to be too expensive. How could she afford the rent, food, bills, school supplies? It was impossible, there was just no way.

'What about getting a job there, in the evenings or on weekends?' Léa asked.

It wasn't recommended. The School of Fine Arts was so strict, the competition so tough, that Jade would have to spend too many hours painting outside of class to be able to work a job as well.

[Longer pause to eat two more oysters.]

They considered different solutions, crazy plans: finding a patron by putting an ad in the local paper, contacting Jade's Polish father (whom they imagined as a wealthy man, the owner of a handball team at least) and asking him to take care of his daughter, finding a squat in Paris to live in, to save on rent.

Of these three solutions, they tried only the first. Léa paid for a short and rather stupid ad. They didn't find a patron, but *La Provence* interviewed Jade and two other students, for a long article on the difficulties that students from the provinces faced trying to study in Paris. At the beginning of the 21st century, when the great capital cities were being revitalised, they became insanely expensive, leaving the elite to take over and excluding everyone else. Gentrification was all the rage in London, New York and Paris. Jade's words and story fit in perfectly with the zeitgeist, not to mention her beautiful cat eyes staring out of the pages in the newspaper.

[Fifth oyster and next-to-the-last-drink.]

Unfortunately, there was still no patron after the article. Jade gave up. Too easily, in Léa's opinion. This was her big chance and she was going to let it slip away forever because of a few miserable francs? Besides, it was too late to get into Avignon University, so she would lose out on a whole year. It was no use talking to her. Jade had given up, so Léa gave up too. They drifted apart again. Léa had started at university and Jade was aimlessly wandering the world. She was supposedly with a man in Marseilles, Toulouse, Barcelona. She no longer lived with her mother, only visited occasionally, and no one knew how she earned her living. Léa always tried to keep in touch with her. She was frightened, worried that something awful would happen to her friend. Once in a while, Jade would call, when things were going well for her; she was working as a model here and there, earning good money. Léa always felt calmer after talking to her. Perhaps it was really true that Jade was discovering an exciting, wonderful world out there, that she was happy for once, while Léa was still living with her parents and wasting her time on boring studies. Painting? Jade wasn't interested in that any more, it was lonely work, she preferred the social life.

Going to England for a year was the perfect solution for Léa; she could show her friend that she too had a thirst for adventure. That's why she invited her to come along for the first week. Léa would pay for her plane ticket, they could both stay in Léa's room. Jade agreed. It was their last chance to regain their former intimacy.

[Sixth and final oyster, and the oysters begin to make themselves known.]

'SO HOW DID IT GO?' I ASKED, SIPPING MY LAST FEW DROPS OF wine, not so much out of thirst as to rid my palate of the aftertaste of mollusk.

'Well, you were there. It was a disaster. Jade was a woman of the world by then, while I was just a little kid who had never left her parents' house before. But as soon as we arrived on campus, the mask dropped. She was in way over her head. I don't know if you remember, but she hid behind me like a little puppy, afraid someone might talk to her, for one thing, because she barely spoke any English. And that hurt her pride. Realising that. Plus the fact that it was so obvious to me. I think that's why she stopped talking to me.'

'When she went back to France, did she ever get back in touch with you?'

'Never. I called her, of course, sent her I don't know how many emails. But then I got a message saying that her email address was no longer valid. I thought the worst. Later I realised she was probably just running away from all her lies, getting herself set up with a new one. She must have changed her name around then, and her email address.'

'Lies? What lies?'

'Is there any truth in anything I've told you? Not much, probably. Do you think the whole story about Paris was true? I think now it was all a lie. That art school accepts ten out of every hundred portfolios they receive, and out of those ten, only one passes the entrance exam. I don't think Jade was that good. I think she took my money, had herself a nice little holiday in Paris, then made up the story about the scholarship to cover up her lie. I, for one, never saw any letters from the school, or any other documents.

I took her at her word. But now, looking back, I have my doubts.'

I wanted to ask her about the name change, the possible connotations that names like Jade and Alice might have, but I had another question to ask first.

'When you were friends, did she ever say anything about wanting to be a mother?'

'Not once. And she told me I was crazy when I said I wanted kids at a young age. And you know what? She was right about that. I was a complete idiot.'

6

THE FIRST BIRTHDAY

*Having children changes your life drastically, and I
really love my life. Children aren't the only things that
bring you gratification and happiness, and it's easier to
give life than to give love.*
CAMERON DIAZ, *INSTYLE* MAGAZINE

UNSTABLE, NARCISSISTIC, EGOCENTRIC, CHARISMATIC, HATEFUL,
out of touch with reality, foolish, overwhelmed by neuroses,
low self-esteem, manipulative, selfish, liar, impulsive, arro-
gant, sneaky, troublemaker, incomprehensible.

All of the above, without a doubt.

But capable of murdering two small children in such a
cold and calculated way? Her own two children, brought into
this world with so much effort, defenceless and tender,
defenceless and loving, defenceless and beautiful? No. Léa
had no doubt about that. No one would have been able to
predict such a thing. But honestly, who could kill a child? No
one. And since no one can, when a child is murdered, we're
all suspects.

'No, no way, absolutely not. But she did, didn't she? She
was capable of doing it. I don't know what to say, but ... all I
know is, pregnancy changes you,' Léa said seriously.

We were at a different bar now, fewer tourists and more
sad little men. It was one of the few places in the city still
open at that hour (half past ten at night!).

'What will happen to her now?'

'Who knows? Anything could happen. She could walk free or get forty years in prison.'

'When's the trial?'

'In the next couple of months, but I don't know for sure.'

'Are you going? To the trial, I mean.'

'Maybe.'

(Of course I would go.)

We drank in silence.

'In my case, it was Fabrice,' said Léa. 'Definitely the result of pregnancy and postpartum depression.'

'Really?' I didn't see the connection.

'Well, you know that when you and I met, I was obsessed with being a mum, I had been since I turned sixteen, really. Totally obsessed. But when I got pregnant, I suddenly started having doubts. Until then, I'd had my head in the sand, I was blind. But then I saw the people around me, like you, for example, and other friends, living it up in London with no real responsibilities, enjoying all the advantages of adult life. Not to mention Albert. I suddenly realised that I had chosen him for his qualities as a father and nothing else. I needed to escape, feel alive, free of the restraints of motherhood. Hence, Fabrice. That's the truth of the matter. If it hadn't been for Fabrice, I probably would have gone back to puking after I ate. Or worse.'

'Fabrice for you, writing for me.'

'And also, when the girls were born,' she went on as if she hadn't heard me, deep in her own introspection. 'I wanted to be with him again. When Laure was born, I resisted it. All the drama was still too fresh in my mind and I had no desire to do it all again. But when Agnès, my youngest, was born, I called him and everything. I didn't care anymore. Even knowing that Albert would never give me a third chance, I didn't care. Fabrice doesn't live here anymore, he moved to a little town in Provence, but he answered my call and we met for a glass of wine at a hotel in the area. He had separated from his wife, but then they got back together. I suppose he had a tough time of it too. I went with the baby, who was barely six weeks old. We didn't go to bed, he wasn't interested at all, he just looked old and sad. He kept looking over his shoulder and checking his watch, obviously wanting to get out of there. I do have some pride. But I'd worked it all out, what time Agnès would nap, where to put the pram, everything.'

'Just as well, huh?'

'I suppose it turned out for the best.'

'But you have to admit there's a huge difference between that and Jade's situation.'

'Of course. I just meant ... Look, before I was a mum, in that naive phase when I still idealised motherhood, I would read stories or see films about mothers who abandoned their children, but they never seemed believable. How could a mother abandon her own children, her greatest treasure? No, surely a mother would make any sacrifice to keep going. I used to believe that shit. Have you seen that Kubrick film, *Eyes Wide Shut*? There's a part where Nicole Kidman confesses to her husband that she had seen a man at a hotel the summer before. The man had glanced at her, that's all, but at that moment she knew without the slightest doubt that she'd throw it all away, her husband, her daughter, her future, leave everything behind to run off with that stranger if he asked her to.'

'Yes, I remember. Then the husband, Tom Cruise, goes crazy and gets lost in the city - New York, right? - and joins in an orgy and ...'

'Right, ha ha ha. The guy goes nuts and spends the whole night trying to rebuild his shattered masculinity, and all because he'd heard something that any woman, any mother has thought or felt at one time or another.'

'True.'

'See? You realise too that there's nothing special about mothers that makes them capable of enduring absolutely anything. Now, I'm not saying it's not terrible, but I do find it believable that some mothers don't abandon their children, but just end it all.'

I DIDN'T SAY SO, DIDN'T WANT HER TO THINK I WAS JUST TRYING to please her, but she was right. My own feelings had been moving along the same lines in the last year. For a while, I had been vaguely interested in Sylvia Plath. I found her poetry impenetrable, but since we were born on the same day, 27 October, for a time I had looked for a deeper connection between us. When I lived in London, I went to see the last house she had lived in, one sunny afternoon in May, on the north side of Regent's Park, an hour and twenty minutes' walk away from work. Of all the big cities in the world, London is probably the nicest for walking in. You'd never know it from a map, where it just looks like a giant oyster with thousands of veins crossing it, a grey mass that will swallow you up forever as soon as you set foot in it, but on the ground there are flowers, parks here and there, low buildings, elegant black cabs, doors painted cheerful colours, and charming pubs. (This is not totally true. Anyone who goes to London will soon learn that there are neighbourhoods south and east of the river that you should never go to, but those get erased from your memory, and all that remains under your feet is the scenic, gracious, civilised London).

It was eight in the evening, the time I usually got off work (my life in London wasn't nearly as free as Léa thought), but the day wasn't over yet. May afternoons in London seem to go on forever, and I walked on, enjoying the smell of spring.

I knew I had arrived when I saw the blue sign on the front of the house. These signs have been hung on houses around the city where notable artists and personalities have lived, but on this house, at 23 Fitzroy Road, the sign had a different poet's name on it. Irish mystic (and father later on in life) William Butler Yeats also lived in that house as a child, nearly a hundred years before Sylvia Plath. Since he got there first, won the Nobel Prize, and had the good grace not to kill himself in the house, he'd got the sign. There was no mention of Sylvia.

Was I disappointed standing there before that ordinary house? White trim, pastel tones. A black wrought iron fence with a sign telling people not to chain their bikes to it. No. Pilgrimages like this one are always internal, since not much happens on the exterior. However, I took a moment to imagine the beautiful Sylvia: I thought about her, getting bread and milk ready for her children on the other side of those walls. She would have spread a thick layer of butter on the toast, as they do in England. Then she would go to the children's room, where they were sleeping. After leaving their breakfast on the night table, she would open their window, seal their door with towels, go downstairs to the kitchen, seal that door as well, turn on the gas, stick her head in the oven, and *goodbye, babies*.

She was thirty.

Her daughter Frieda was almost three, and Nicholas was only thirteen months old. I could imagine Frieda the next morning, holding a spoonful of cold milk to her brother's mouth, getting a piece of bread. But probably the people who found Sylvia's body got there before the children woke up. I want to believe that.

The poet's two labours had been quick and easy home births, both in other houses, not the one I was visiting, and both described in magnificent detail in her frequent letters to her mother in the U.S. The births of both children had brought tremendous happiness to Sylvia – briefly, but without the slightest hint of postpartum depression. She had a burst of creativity then, too. She locked herself in her study, taking turns looking after the children with her husband, Ted Hughes, whom feminists later repeatedly targeted. After the second birth, she wrote *Ariel*, her most famous work. On 4 March, 1962, six weeks after Nicholas was born, she wrote this note to her mother, which fills me with wonder and shame: 'I am managing to get about two and a bit more hours in my study in the mornings and hope to make it four when I can face getting up at six, which I hope will be as soon as Nicholas stops waking for a night feeding'. And then in April, 'I never dreamed it was possible to get such joy out of babies.

I do think mine are special'. And on 15 June, 'I don't know when I've been so happy or felt so well'.

Ecstasy in darkness.

But later, always and forever, nothing but darkness.

I spent five or six minutes in front of the house, and saw a couple of residents coming and going. I imagined the former single-family home now divided into tiny apartments. I didn't want to prolong my visit too much, and arouse suspicion.

I tenderly imagined Sylvia's final minutes, the kisses she gave her daughter and son. Her immeasurable love for her children made her suicide even harder to imagine, to my way of thinking. Even if only for their sake, shouldn't she have carried on? Was the prospect of watching Frieda and Nicholas grow up not enough to make life worth living? A few more years at least, until the children reached adolescence?

Apparently not.

After Plath's suicide, Ted Hughes had another daughter with his lover, Assia Wevill. Although they lived together and Assia took care of the orphaned Frieda and Nicholas, they never married and Ted never officially recognised his new daughter, a girl they named Shura, who was as beautiful as her mother. But life was not easy. Assia was endlessly haunted by Sylvia's ghost until finally, on 23rd March, 1969, she too turned on the gas. But Assia gave a new twist to the family tradition Sylvia had started. Before she lit the gas, she gave Shura sleeping pills and laid her down on a mattress on the kitchen floor. After she lit the gas, she lay down at her daughter's side. She held her tight. Until everything went dark. Shura was four years old. Assia was forty-one, a half-Jewish woman who had escaped the Nazis as a child.

Psychiatry uses the term *extended suicide* for such cases.

Sylvia's son, Nicholas Hughes, also killed himself in 2009 in Alaska. That's how far the blonde poet's suicide extended, the family tradition. All the way to Alaska.

Uluru.

Dingo.

Rhodesia.

Alaska.

'IF SHE HAD KILLED HERSELF AFTERWARDS ...' LÉA COULD still read my mind.

'... we'd feel nothing but pity now, and wouldn't even think about the kids.'

'Exactly.'

'But she didn't kill herself, dammit, she's still alive and living with what she did. That's the worst.'

'That's the worst.'

We stared at the bottle of wine.

I WANTED TO KNOW MORE, BUT AT THE SAME TIME, I DIDN'T want to know more. It seemed that instead of shedding light on the mystery of Jade/Alice, Léa's words simply added fuel to the fire. And I couldn't do anything with the ashes. I had a clearer picture of Jade though; Léa is bright and knows how to get to the heart of the matter, but what lies in that heart? Not much, it seems. A troubled teenager, a girl raised in difficult circumstances, suffering from one or two undiagnosed mental illnesses. The portrait is hardly unique, bordering on cliché. But no matter how well defined, the portrait does not explain what she did, *the act*, the truth.

Perhaps I needed to take a step back from reality. Move into the realm of fiction, in the hopes that at least a piece of the truth might shine through.

Or maybe we just needed to go to a different bar.

The answer to that question is always 'yes', but we were in Avignon and it was late, so nightclubs were our only option.

Léa suggested we walk along the Rhône to see the famous bridge. It would remind her of her student days, when she used to come here with a book to study in the sun. She had never come to the city centre since she had moved to the suburbs, and had almost forgotten the walls, the murmur of the water, the broken bridge.

'How do you picture it?' I asked her after we had walked in silence for a few minutes. 'What was her state of mind that day, by the tub? Rage? Alienation? Indifference?'

'It's something I've thought about a lot.' She had paused a long while before responding, but of course she knew exactly what I was talking about. 'Which hypothesis is the most horrifying? Rage, we can understand, the moment when someone loses control, is pushed a little too far and explodes. Were they crying? Would they not calm down? Did she just lose it? Maybe it was an irrational impulse that made her do something that can't be undone. It might have been. But what if she did it calmly, determinedly? What if she undressed the babies, put one in the bath, and then gently pushed its head under the water? And when the baby clung to life and waved its arms and legs, eyes wide open, aware of what its mother was doing even as its little face turned blue ... What if, even with all this, she kept going until the end?'

'And then did the same thing with the second baby as well.'

'Who was first? Definitely the boy.'

'I think it was the girl.'

I don't know why I said that. It seemed terribly flippant. I felt my stomach clench, my throat tighten. I moved as far away from Léa as I could and threw up by the river. My anxiety floated away towards the Mediterranean.

'Classic. Your Avignon ritual,' Léa laughed.

'I bet it was the oysters,' I answered in the same tone.

But really, I was crying, so I stood for a while in the dark, disgusted with myself. There were some things I couldn't talk about, which is why I had to write about them. Even if it wasn't right.

BACK AT THE HOTEL, PERHAPS IN THE SAME ROOM WHERE LÉA had committed her adultery, I opened my notebook and tried to write down everything the night had revealed. Then I went over to the basin to squeeze out some milk, but almost nothing came. The body adapts quickly. It was three in the morning when I turned off the light for six hours of restless sleep, in a complete but unfamiliar solitude, alone for the first time in a long time.

My stomach was still unsettled the next morning, so I got straight onto the motorway and didn't waste any time on breakfast. I stopped the car at an *aire de repos* before the border. I ordered a large *café au lait* and an even larger chocolate *macaron* and then looked at some toys for a bit. I chose a wooden train, a classic, which was absurdly expensive, but seemed appropriate for my little Viking, who would be celebrating his first birthday the next day.

IN THE FOLLOWING DAYS AND WEEKS, AND FOR THE FIRST time since giving birth, my thoughts were far away from Jade. I didn't open my notebook again, and barely even thought about my meeting with Léa. I felt ill, and had no desire to eat oysters ever again, or revisit any of the notes I had written so far. I had thought that meeting with Léa, getting a first-hand portrait of Jade, would inspire me, but I couldn't have been more wrong. In fact, that night in Avignon had the totally opposite effect, though I didn't regret my getaway. It had been wonderful to be together again and enjoy the evening.

The rest of our holiday went well. My 24-hour absence hadn't traumatised anyone. We adjusted to the hotel's schedule, Erik was losing his fear of the water, and we had a lovely birthday party for him, inviting a few other kids from the hotel for birthday cake by the swimming pool. As soon as we got back home, Niclas' parents arrived and we did a lot of walking with them. They seemed to have arrived with a desire to climb every mountain in Bizkaia. When they left, I was exhausted, both from climbing mountains and from hosting. But my exhaustion was purely physical. My head was clear, my mind was sharp, nothing was troubling me, there were no storm clouds on the horizon, and I was enjoying the baby more than ever. He had just started walking, and tottered towards me laughing, arms open wide and, with my heart overflowing with pride and love, I thought about how quickly children bloom before our eyes and how little we realise it, always up to our ears in the task of raising them.

The days flew by, it was almost September and I still couldn't muster any desire to write. What if that desire never returned? What if I never finished the book? And would anyone even want to read it anyway? What if I would be doing society a favour by never writing it, consigning it to the rubbish bin forever? What if I never wrote again?

But I had taken a leave of absence, a decision that affected the whole family, and I couldn't just throw it all away and claim it had been nothing but a whim, a crazy idea. And, getting into murkier waters: could I really give up writing forever? What would happen to that part of my identity if it were silenced and quashed? And on a more mundane level, wouldn't my giving up writing be proof that the people who thought I didn't deserve the prize were right? Well, no one knew exactly what I was writing about; maybe I could reshape the project. Perhaps I could use the documentation I had collected so far to write an essay that would include my own experience as a mother. But would I be able to write anything interesting about it, besides percentiles, teeth and constipation? An ambivalent mix of complaints and affection, page after page, exhaustion and love, disappointment and absolute tenderness, harsh guilt and immoderate pride, all this over and over, again and again, until the reader gives up in disgust?

I thought it would do me good to go back to work. My job is somewhat creative – as creative as developing communication plans for dental clinics allows – and I thought my daily activities might give me some perspective (what perspective? no idea, but some perspective) for future writing projects.

I resolved to put all my work on the back burner until then. *Sine die.* The inclination to finish the book would come in its own good time.

But then, on the last day of August, we were spending the last day of our holiday at an outdoor café, with Erik at our feet picking up napkins and olive pits, when I opened a paper and read a piece of news that changed all my plans: Alice Espanet's trial would be starting soon. Jury selection would take place in mid-September, and the trial would start a few days later.

It was like a slap in the face. I hadn't expected it to start so soon. I thought I would have more time. At least another year, according to my calculations. But no, it had been fourteen months since *the act*; the investigation must have gone smoothly. I saw as clear as day that I had to be there, had to follow each and every step, see Jade/Alice's face, hear her words, examine her every expression. It was an opportunity I couldn't miss, and all the signs said I had to be there. The news had caught me at a low point in my writing; it couldn't be a coincidence. The key to the whole story lay in those days at the trial, those statements. I knew this without the slightest doubt and suddenly, but also naturally, I found myself gripped by the same obsession that had ruled my mental state a year before. Right there in the café. I was grateful for its return. The only problem was that they were expecting me back at work the next day. I had only a few hours to make the necessary arrangements at home and at work so I could extend my leave.

My bank account, at the end of the summer and after Niclas' unexpected dental implants, held €4,407.

PART II
VIOLENCE

1
KILLING CHILDREN

It's a hard world for little things.
LILIAN GISH IN *THE NIGHT OF THE HUNTER*

LADIES AND GENTLEMEN OF THE JURY, FIRST AND FOREMOST, breathe in, breathe out, relax your jaws. The best thing you can do right now is to stop being shocked. What you need now is a little historical perspective. Because, ladies and gentlemen, this is nothing new. Quite the contrary, it is as old as humanity: children, babies, newborns have always been killed. Why? There might be many reasons, but this is basically why, so listen carefully: it is easy to kill a child. Because they are small, because they are weak, because they are unable to organise themselves and demand their rights, rise up, sharpen the guillotine, return the blow. This is the truth, and I will say it again: it is easy to kill children. Much easier than killing a strong man, a powerful man. So easy that (just think about it!) you don't actually have to *do* anything at all. While abortion requires *action* (whether it's turpentine or a rusty, unsterilised hanger up the uterus), infanticide requires only *omission*. Don't protect it, don't feed it, don't take care of it, leave it in the forest, shut it in a wardrobe, forget you put it there. Done.

And not only that, ladies and gentlemen. Historically speaking, killing children has rarely had any consequences. Why? Because children have always been considered the property of adults. This is the case, even today, to a large extent. With property (whether slave, woman, or child) we have the right to do whatever we want. Is this not so?

A look at history through the ages shows us the same thing: in the absence of reliable contraceptives, the most basic way of controlling the birth rate was infanticide. Is this not logical, if we think about it coldly? While abortion was a high-risk practice for the mother (as it was until at least the middle of the 20th century, and continues to be in many parts of the world), abandoning a newborn in the forest did the new mother no physical harm at all. In ancient Rome, if a family wanted to adopt a baby, they went directly to the rubbish tip, where they could always find a newborn and, with a bit of luck, one that was still alive.

Another significant reason, century after century, has been eugenics. Greek physician Soranus of Ephesus, considered the father of gynaecology, wrote a brief guide on how to distinguish children who were worth raising from those who were not. If they didn't meet certain criteria, then it was better to throw the little ones in the river. It takes too much energy to raise a child. We need to be sure that it will be worth it. There will always be more children. Healthier. Stronger. There will always be more. Children are like that.

In Sparta, this practice was taken to its limits: the State itself took responsibility for the inspection of all newborn babies, of all new potential soldiers and, if necessary, their systematic disposal.

Thousands of years later (for history has its wormholes), similar practices were applied in Nazi Germany, always for the purpose of optimising the Aryan race. The premature, the crippled, the retarded were all transferred as soon as they were born to wards called *Kinderfachabteilungen*, and there, a small dose of phenobarbital (provided by Bayer Laboratories) was enough to erase all those defective little Germans from history. The paediatricians, midwives and nurses of the Reich were forced to report the births of 'special' children. These medical professionals received payment for each such child they identified, and they did their job so efficiently that, in only a few years, they brought about the genocide of more than 10,000 infants. Meanwhile, abortion was illegal, and any woman who did it, or planned to do it, would get the death penalty.

But let us stick to the teleological evolution of history, ladies and gentlemen, for I would not want to perplex you with too many leaps and bounds.

In Rome as well, this practice was protected by law, at least until the arrival of Christianity. According to the primitive Roman Law of the Twelve Tables, the *pater familias* could have his child killed if it were born with a deformity. Until the 4th century, infanticide was very common in Rome if the newborn could not be supported, if the parents did not want to support it, or if it unfortunately happened to be a girl. *If it's a girl, get rid of it*, wrote one wealthy merchant on a business trip to his pregnant wife. (Fortunately, only two countries today still follow the custom of getting rid of newborn girls: China and India. Unfortunately, nearly half of the world's population is concentrated in those two countries).

The killing of children has often been a way to satisfy the whims of the gods. In the Mayan jungle, in all-powerful Carthage, in Celtic lands, in the most frozen corners of Siberia, here, there and everywhere, infanticide has taken the form of an offering to the gods. Although, in the end it was only a macabre joke, Abraham found God's request neither particularly strange, nor particularly scandalous; he simply gathered up the wood, took up the axe, and bound Isaac, his terrified and trembling son.

Infanticide has also been carried out on the whims of kings. An insane strategy of statesmen. Some organised the mass killing of all children under the age of two, without taking into account the ruinous demographic consequences: the pharaoh in the time of Moses, for example, or the later copycat Herod the Great, King of Judea. Poor little innocents.

But breathe, ladies and gentlemen: as history progressed, society began to condemn these practices. Contrary to general belief, any time in the past was always worse, always, always, always, at least until now. Constantine, the first Christian Roman Emperor, rejected infanticide, and in the Council of Constantinople a revolutionary idea took hold: infanticide is a type of homicide. What? But they're only children! Even so.

In any case, the conduct of the Catholic church is paradoxical in this regard: on the one hand, it condemns infanticide; on the other, it condemns children born out of wedlock to a life of misery. Indeed, until the 18th century, bastard children had no rights and no laws to protect them; they were fugitives, pariahs, pestilent, condemned to bear the sin of their mothers for life.

And what about the other religion? Well, the Qur'an 17:31 explicitly forbids the killing of children. *Do not kill your children for fear of want. We will provide for them and for you. Surely killing them is a great sin.*

And here we come to another important reason for infanticide. One child, one mouth. Thus, another child, another mouth ... among too many hungry mouths. God, we are told, will provide.

But is that provision truly guaranteed? Anglican cleric Malthus wrote that the potential for growth of the human population was much greater than the capacity of the Earth to produce human sustenance. The logical consequence is catastrophe, a *Malthusian catastrophe*, and all because children insist on continuing to be born into the world. Reading between the lines of Malthus, the solution is clear; it's a matter of survival. Since the instinct to reproduce is uncontrollable, we must instead control the number of mouths that are born, that is to say, to close them forever. But, but ..., but what then, Reverend, of the divine mandate to *be fruitful and multiply*? A few decades earlier, another cleric named Jonathan Swift recommended that the poor of Ireland sell their children – preferably those under a year of age – to the rich as food, so that all those infants who would otherwise die of hunger could become fricassee or ragout-style delicacies. A practical solution, to be sure, and ultimately a win-win situation, as they say.

But let us leave the realm of satire. The looks on your faces tell me that this is no time for such frivolity. When all is said and done, there are also well-documented cases of mothers who ate their own children. And not that long ago, either: in the Ukraine for example, in the time of Stalin and the great famine. We don't need any more details, however, enough is enough, but do keep this idea in mind: we are moving forward, our sensibilities are becoming more refined, the birth of humanitarianism is nigh. At some point, the law will stop protecting infanticide, even in the case of illegitimate children.

This does not mean that infanticide will end. It simply means that, under the threat of harsh punishment, it will be done in secret.

This change is not insignificant, however, and now we arrive at the case at hand: infanticide moves from being systematic to being primarily the act of desperate mothers. From the Middle Ages to the 19th century, the most common reason given for killing a baby had to do with *honour*. The character of Gretchen in Goethe's *Faust* is an example of this, and has been a literary archetype since the end of the 18th century: Faust wins sexual favours from Gretchen through his deal with the devil, Gretchen gives birth and, in an attempt to hide her dishonour, drowns the newborn without a second thought. As was the custom, the woman is sentenced to death for her crime. Faust cannot accept this – he is in love, after all – and asks for the devil's help once more, to have his seduced (raped?) lover released from prison. But it's too late for her, she has already lost her mind because of what she did. She refuses to escape and dies in Faust's arms. Another lost soul. Another eternal punishment. We find the same story in Catalan literature: Caterina Albert, under the pen name of Víctor Català, wrote the monologue *The Child Killer*, for which she won the Jocs Florals prize in 1898. The story is very similar: seduction, sex, pregnancy, immediate disappearance of the man, devastating arrival of the child, desperation, millstone, the grinding of tiny bones, the involvement of the authorities, and the madhouse for life.

Let us take a leap now, ladies and gentlemen of the jury, from romantic literature to the reality of Victorian London, if you will still grant me the honour of your attention. In that dirty proletarian metropolis, maids, for example, knew they stood to lose their job if they rejected the *seduction* of the gentleman of the house. Unfortunately, if, as a result of that seduction – rape, that is – they became pregnant, they would be turned out of the house. (This is not entirely true, however: some men, such as Karl Marx, convinced their maid to give the child up for adoption. There have always been a few good men). With the maid out on the street, marginalised, no resources whatsoever, and bearing within her the growing *dishonour* resulting from her *seduction*, it is not difficult to imagine the dark fate awaiting the newborn.

Queen Victoria herself had to intervene, so that all those fallen women would not receive the death penalty. And this takes us back to infanticide as a legal exception. Infanticide is *not* homicide, at least not if it's the mother who commits it. It cannot be the same thing.

This exception is still reflected in the penal codes of various countries today. In Spain, for example, in a law that was in effect until 1995, infanticide was considered a different crime. In the words of the law, *a mother who kills her newborn to hide her dishonour shall receive the minimum prison sentence.* Modernised variations do not mention dishonour, but do mention *the mother who kills her newborn as a result of the emotional distress of the post-partum period*. Sentence: six months to six years. In earlier versions of the law, the mother's parents – the grandparents – may also be the authors of the infanticide. But not the father; for the father, it will always be plain homicide.

From 1995 onwards, the concept of infanticide disappears in Spain, and a mother who kills her child can be charged with homicide. Not so in other countries, however. In Canada, for example. In this exemplary American country, a mother will be committing infanticide if she kills her child under the age of one, as a result of an altered mental state due to pregnancy, childbirth or lactation (?). And she is therefore exempt from punishment. She only needs some proof that she was not of sound mind, proof that she lost her marbles due to her pregnancy, childbirth or lactation. And what proof is generally offered? The fact that she killed her child! What could possibly be clearer? With this perfect tautology, a mother who has killed her child gets out of jail free in Canada. The nature of this crime has been called into question in recent years, on the basis that the law reeks of Victorianism. Nevertheless, it remains in effect today. A law worth keeping in mind, in my humble opinion.

But let us cut to the chase, ladies and gentlemen of the jury. This is no small task you have before you. Therefore, you need to have a clear understanding. Children have always been killed, even today, even though we are more shocked by it nowadays. And indeed, we are very shocked by it. The child molester, the kidnapper in the park, the predatory child killer, these are the worst monsters imaginable. And yet, the massacre of the innocents goes on, as you must all surely know. In the summer of 2014, the Israeli army assassinated 400 children in Gaza, those twenty-five miles of cursed land. In Mexico City, a child under five is killed every other day. In every attack in Syria, children account for 27% of the dead. Casualties among children are always mentioned to illustrate the horrors of war. But this prevents neither the killing of children, nor the wars. The image of a drowned three-year-old led to the drama of the refugee crisis being splashed across the front pages of the newspapers for several days, in the summer of 2015. However, this did not open the doors to Europe more than a tiny crack, which was quickly shut again.

Okay, you didn't come here to talk about wars and bombings. Nor is there any need to. When there is no war, in the peaceful and civilised West, right here in our own country, the risk to children lies in our homes. In Europe, on average, incidents of domestic violence kill around 3,500 children every year.

Although Euripides tells the story of a woman who killed her children to hurt the husband who abandoned her, we can say without any fear of contradiction that the modern-day Medea is a man: in the last decade in Spain, some fifty divorcing or recently divorced fathers killed their own childen, hoping through those murders to destroy their mothers forever. Not without reason, most modern interpretations focus on Medea's masculine traits, or more specifically, on the conflict between the masculine and the feminine: the masculine side that calls for action, terrible but in some sense also heroic, the sacrifice of children for a greater cause, while the feminine, maternal, caring side calls for the opposite, and pleads for the children to be allowed to live.

Euripides shows us that the masculine side prevails.

In Vincenzo Bellini's opera *Norma*, on the other hand, Gallic druid Norma steps back after approaching her children, knife in hand. Betrayed by their father, she sees no other way out. In the end, her feminine side wins and she lets the little ones live.

And you will say to me, with good reason, that even feminine mothers kill their children. Of course, because if not, what are you all doing here, on these benches, in this solemn chamber, charged with this tremendous responsibility? It's not something that's mentioned often, at least not explicitly, but one of the pieces of advice that is always given to new mothers is this: if you have suicidal thoughts, or thoughts about harming your baby, ask for help. The midwife says this to every woman who has just given birth. It's also mentioned in the information pamphlet published by the Health Service. One week after giving birth, when you go for your first check-up, the midwife will ask you again: how are you feeling? Any disturbing thoughts? And she'll check over the baby, looking for any signs of abuse. There are good reasons for this.

Esteemed members of the jury, most honourable ladies and gentlemen. Eugenics, revenge, Malthusianism, seduction, dishonour, poverty, utter destitution, unwed mothers, bastards and the sins of their parents, postpartum emotional distress, extended suicide, postpartum depression, madness caused by lactation, madness, madness.

I know.

We cannot understand it.

You cannot understand it, is that not so?

These mothers break all the moulds.

This mother, specifically.

This is no small task you have before you.

I shall stay here, hidden in the audience, lying in wait. I wouldn't want to be in your shoes. I'm better off where I am.

2

JADE/ALICE

*One often hears that women 'have bellyaches';
true indeed, a hostile element is locked inside
them: the species is eating away at them.*
SIMONE DE BEAUVOIR, *THE SECOND SEX*

NO ONE COULD DENY THAT ALICE IS A BEAUTIFUL WOMAN.

Her eyes are alluring, she has a certain aura about her. The proper proportions to her perfect countenance. Proper angulation between spine and shoulders. The gift of gliding unheavily through space.

Therefore, undeniably, everything is easier. In the crib, in the classroom, at the bar, at the office, in the queue at the supermarket and, needless to say, on the bench of the accused.

Pandas surely owe their survival into the present day to being so cute. They eat only bamboo, they have a life expectancy of 12 years but don't begin to reproduce until the age of 7, and the females are fertile for only five days a year. Furthermore, if, by chance, twins are born, the mother focuses on only one, condemning the other to death. According to Darwinism, they should have disappeared long ago. But, since they remind us of the teddy bears of our childhood, we take good care of them. There's no other possible reason.

Alice, are you a panda?

A soft, warm, black and white panda, of course.

You had two cubs and you had to kill them both.

What a lovely panda you are.

At first glance, at least.

Then some people may begin to peek behind the Wizard of Oz's curtain. For beauty, in principle and unless proven otherwise, is always suspect. The myth of the *femme fatale* has brought a risk of mortal danger to beauty. *La belle dame sans merci*, as the romantics would call it.

Alice has chestnut hair, beautiful, wavy medium-length hair that she wears loose. With the right dress, she would be a perfect model for a Pre-Raphaelite portrait. Pale face, red lips, enigmatic expression. Beautiful. And merciless, apparently. She lined her eyes this morning too, just a little. Moderately dressed, in the way of the accused: black pencil skirt, white blouse with a large bow at the neck, no heels. Everything in moderation, everything carefully planned out with her lawyer. They tried putting her hair up, but it made her face look too stark. Better as it is.

Hands on the table. A blank piece of paper and a black pen in front of her. She does not touch them. She keeps her hands on the table, seemingly relaxed. Looking like she has nothing to hide. Carmela Basaguren, her lawyer, whispers something to her. Alice nods, still looking straight ahead.

I won't deny that I'm on tenterhooks.

Here we are at last, the two of us, again. I see you. Will you see me? Will you remember me? I hope not.

Alice, Jade, what have you been doing since the last time I saw you, in a dorm room on a small campus in western England? How did you end up sitting here, in a court in Gasteiz, with me in the sixth row? And what awaits you in the future, if you even have a future? Are you thinking about it, or do you deny the future, no today and no tomorrow, now that you've lost compass, calendar, clock?

The judge in his robes. And, on the judge's right, the jury. They look more sad than stern. They will decide what to do with you. On the judge's left, the prosecutors, the attorneys, you, seated in a perfect semicircle.

What to do with you, Alice; what to do with you, Jade?

Humanity has been imaginative with its defendants; the answers have been numerous and varied. Hard labour in a quarry, in galleys, in the trenches, torment and torture, the walk of shame, dismemberment by horses, brazen bulls, head on a pike, breast amputation, Siberia, Guyana, Australia, Socrates' hemlock, fire, sword, gallows, chasm, garotte, guillotine, electric chair, lethal injection.

No, Jade, no, Alice. Nothing like that for you, you can be sure of that.

The criminal justice system has evolved here among us. The body is not punished now; it is the soul that is punished. The crime is not judged now; it is the spirit that is judged.

Nevertheless, Alice has a body, and that body may see forty years of prison. Forty years of frisking, showers, standing in lines, head counts, yard hours, eleven steps forward and eleven steps back, everything measured, letters, aluminium trays, lights that go on and off on someone else's schedule, walls, fences, boundaries. The body there. The soul, who knows where. The spirit. ...

And yet Alice's spirit can't be caught, it leaps from one member of the jury to another without anyone noticing.

Now it's fled to the judge's bench and slips in among his papers, now to the prosecutor's robes, with a skip and a jump.

Her body, however, is here. In a specific place, in this prominent position. In front of everyone. It's not just any body. If she was beautiful at twenty-one then, some eleven years later, the woman is even more beautiful. She looks as if she were made of porcelain, fired hard in the kiln and still strong. How much of an influence will this have? I see her in profile; she faces the jury, hour after hour, day after day. Those cat eyes. The dance of her eyelashes. Her perfect proportions. A panda. She's not hiding.

I ALSO SEE RITXI, THOUGH I HAD FORGOTTEN ABOUT HIM AT first, drawn to the chiaroscuro portrait that is Alice. He sits in the front row, with two other men and a woman of similar age. His bald spot was inconspicuous in the photos I had seen here and there. Or perhaps it's simply a result of the stress of this past dramatic year. He hardly moves, he's a statue. Every once in a while he turns his head to whisper something to the friends at his side and I can confirm that it is he: wine entrepreneur, Led Zeppelin fan, father without children.

Silence reigns in the chamber, and I think it must be the tension of the opening moments. It's the first day of class; from now on, moods will calm and procedures will relax. For the moment, I too am trying not to make a sound, not to move, not to look at Alice too directly. What would happen if she looked over to the sixth row and recognised my face?

Could she search her memory and place me in another time and place, far from here, another era? What would she think? That I am a ghost from the past, brought here to remind her of the time back when she was Jade, in a judicial ploy to break the accused once and for all? She doesn't look, she won't look, and even if she does see me, she won't look for more than half a second; she's got more important things on her mind.

Everything is sterile and follows clear procedures. The judge – a completely ordinary-looking man in his fifties – gives instructions, mostly to the jury. He seems bored. The cynicism of a man who has seen it all. Perhaps it's his way of showing his neutrality, refined through years of experience. Five women and four men. A delegation of good citizens. I feel for them. They look to be between twenty-five and sixty years old. Some take notes, just to be doing something. They're scared, but excited as well. At least they'll have something to talk about at home, and that's always something to be grateful for.

So far, no one has mentioned the children, though *the act* has been mentioned more than once.

Then the judge calls Alice Espanet to the stand. I didn't think it would happen this soon. I wasn't ready for it, just as I wasn't ready for the trial itself to start so early. I feel the first serious ripple in the audience as Alice stands in front of the microphone and states her name.

Her voice, her appearance, her pronunciation, her delivery, her body language, her clothes, the distribution of dramatic effects, the balance between emotion and cold reason, the apt use of metaphors, the sound, unassailable, definitive conclusion. All of these matter in this piece of theatre, as in any piece of theatre.

What is my first impression? That she's gotten off to an excellent start. She speaks Spanish very well, though with a strong accent. She pauses to find the right words. She doesn't lose her nerve, even in the face of the prosecutor's pointed questions. The prosecutor looks like a parrot, big nose for a beak and dyed chestnut hair for flashy plumage. Her voice is grating, a good three tones higher than her natural speaking voice. Beside her, Alice is the mistress of her own vocal cords.

Her worst nightmare, says Alice, mother without children, when asked to describe *the act* in her own words. The cry of the demonic spirit. One that she heard from the beginning, and that's why she refused to be alone with the children: because she knew that one day she would give in to the spirit; it would catch her in a weak moment and bear her away. But she felt better at the time of the events, or thought she did. Painting helped. And so she began spending time alone with the children. Just a few hours here and there. The calm afternoon hours. And then, when she least expected it, the shadow of the demon took over. She couldn't remember the details. Everything went blank all of a sudden. When the dense fog cleared with the last breath of air, the children were on the bed, soaked, cold. She tried to get them to nurse, both of them, though she had never tried before. But she saw that it was impossible. She remembers nothing more until she woke up in the hospital.

And that's where the spell broke for me. There was nothing but a small grey man behind the curtain, moving levers.

What was the point of this cheap and confused recitation of clichés? Nightmare? Demon? Fog? Amnesia? Alice, Jade, I expected better of you. I don't know why, but I did. I hoped to believe you, to understand you, to have a vivid and detailed account.

Why do we assign aesthetic value to murder, to murderers? Is not the criminal always a miserable creature, abhorrent and wretched? Why so many novels, films, television series? Why do we feel the need to intellectualise? Why must we swallow so many oysters?

What we have here is a killer. Look at her. She is as amorphous as an oyster, and inspires only pity, or disgust.

But I seem to be the only one standing in front of this broken mirror.

Two members of the jury wipe their tears discreetly. The whole chamber is frozen. After making sure there are no more questions, the judge sends Alice back to her seat. She rises, tugs her pencil skirt back down to her knees and returns to her lawyer's side. Calmly, eyes to the floor. Carmela Basaguren touches her shoulder reassuringly, just for a second.

The judge announces a fifteen-minute break.

IT BECAME A ROUTINE FOR ME. THE BUREAUCRATIC PROCEDURES, the legal jargon, the black robes, it all helped me see things from a distance and to act as professionally as the law students. I arrived on time, took my usual seat in the sixth row, avoided the journalists – from time to time I saw one that looked familiar – and waited in the queue at the coffee machine without speaking to anyone. I took lots of notes. By the fourth day of the trial, I had already filled half of the black notebook I had bought for the purpose. I was spending quite a lot of money on petrol, round-trip tolls and blue zone parking. The sessions always went on until two o'clock or half past. If they finished at two, I had time for a quick bite of potato omelette at the bar behind the court building before heading back to Bilbao. On more than one occasion Carmela Basaguren was there too, having a glass of white wine. If we got out later, I skipped lunch and went straight home to Erik, who had started staying at school until half past three in the new school year. In that case, I made the trip with a stomach full of coffee from the machine, always feeling slightly queasy.

I was coming to understand that trials are a contest of stories. Basically, there are two opposing stories, very different from each other, that are in effect two artefacts obtained by combining the same elements – the mythemes – in different ways. Don't hire a lawyer, hire a good writer. Because it's not the truth that will win, but the person who tells the best story, the most coherent and believable one. In other words, the most mythological story, the one best able to fit the world view of the jurors.

The prosecution presents a piece of evidence and provides an interpretation.

The defence proposes a different way of interpreting the same piece of evidence.

The jury has to decide which one to go with.

Which story and which body and which spirit to believe.

I NEVER WROTE HER A LETTER, AND I WAS HAPPY WITH THAT decision. I continued watching from the sidelines without her knowing I was there; the role of voyeur suited me perfectly, and I intended to keep playing it.

Besides, by then I knew I would never find the truth in Alice's words.

A BUNCH OF POLICEMEN TESTIFIED. INSTEAD OF STATING their names before the microphone, they gave their collar numbers. It was clear that they were used to being in court, and they did not seem particularly disturbed by the grimness of the case. The first to testify were all from the division of public security, since they had been the first to respond to Mélanie's call for help. They all noted the calm demeanour of the accused, the lack of vital signs in the children, the meticulous order of the house, the hysteria of the nanny.

'When you arrived at the house, did the accused demonstrate any awareness of what she had done?' the prosecutor asked again and again, in her unpleasant voice.

She did seem to be aware, yes, all four of them said, since the woman kept repeating that 'they're fine now,' as if she had achieved a goal or completed a mission.

'In your experience, is that sort of calm typical in someone who has just committed a murder?' countered Basaguren.

No, said the first policeman, but every case is different. The suspects are usually more nervous, exchanges with the police tend to be more chaotic, the scene of the crime is generally messier. But in this case, there was a huge contrast between the events and the reaction of the accused. The second policeman, however, tried to stress that sometimes suspects in a state of shock will behave like that.

'Do you mean to say that Mrs Espanet was in a state of shock?'

'I'd say so, yes.'

'Excuse me, sir, but are you a psychiatrist?'

'A psychiatrist? No, no, but after so many years of experience ...'

'A simple yes or no will be sufficient.'

Agent 4182 fell silent and Carmela had no more questions, seemingly satisfied. But the two psychiatrists who treated Alice at the Santiago Hospital both agreed that she was in a state of shock. Disorientation, amnesia, denial ... she showed all the typical symptoms the whole time she was at the hospital.

The testimony of the psychiatrist who had treated Alice all year was very lengthy. He was a grey-haired Belgian of a certain age, who had earned many titles and honours and was wholly respectable. Doctor Leclercq. He spoke French with Alice during her sessions but had worked in Barcelona for a long time. At Carmela Basaguren's request, he gave us a lecture on postpartum depression and psychosis, a topic upon which he had carried out pioneering research in the 1970s in his own country.

'THE MOST COMMON MANIFESTATION IS WHAT WE CALL THE baby blues. Although 80% of new mothers experience it, it's not considered pathological. It's caused by a hormonal imbalance following childbirth, and can be aggravated by fatigue and lack of sleep, but usually goes away on its own after a few weeks. The symptoms? Most particularly, deep feelings of sadness. The new mother may cry for no apparent reason, or feel like the situation is overwhelming: "I'm not fit for this, "it's too much for me"... She may feel anxious at times, or guilty. But, as mentioned, the mother generally returns to a healthy emotional balance on her own. A couple of weeks, a couple of months ... If the symptoms continue or get worse, then it's time to see a doctor. The mother's medical history will be taken, a psychological examination will be carried out, and various analyses will be done to rule out physical causes. At this point, we're talking about postpartum depression, and that's a serious thing. It's usually treated with a combination of psychotropic drugs and therapy, but it's not easily cured. It could take years for the woman to fully recover. And it can become even worse: the depression can develop into psychosis, in which case there is a high risk that the woman will harm herself or her child, and then hospitalisation is usually the only recourse, with round-the-clock care.'

When the lawyer for the defence asked why Alice hadn't told a doctor about her condition, the psychiatrist didn't hesitate. Unfortunately, her condition was not at all un-common. According to various studies carried out in Europe and the United States, the percentage of mothers who seek help for their depression is very low, only about 15%.

'This illness is still taboo today,' said Dr Leclercq. 'We must not forget the societal pressure placed upon mothers. For a great number of women, it's very difficult to admit that being a mother does not bring happiness, and that in fact, they feel depressed. It's hard to admit it to themselves, to their families, and to the authorities (doctors are authorities, after all).'

'So the road from depression to psychosis is not necessarily a straight one?'

'Exactly,' said the psychiatrist. 'But in Mrs Espanet's case, it's quite clear.'

'In your opinion, then, Alice was suffering from post-partum psychosis?'

'Yes, that's correct.'

'And upon what exactly do you base your diagnosis?'

'Well ... the effects are obvious ...' For the first time, the Belgian doctor appeared ruffled.

'Could you be more specific, please?'

'As with any form of psychosis, this involves a loss of touch with reality. A mother with depression may have ego-dystonic thoughts about harming the baby.'

'Ego-dystonic?' asked Carmela Basaguren, as if she did not already know the meaning of the word.

'That means that the impulse is at odds with her way of thinking, causing a sort of cognitive dissonance that, in turn, provokes feelings of anxiety and guilt. But in a state of psychosis, the idea of harming the baby is ego-syntonic: the thought is not disturbing, on the contrary, the subject sees clearly that she must do it and at that moment, this does not seem problematic. And often, she acts on that thought.'

'I understand, but let me ask you once again: how can you be sure that what Mrs Espanet suffered was indeed psychosis?'

'It's quite clear in the way she talks about the events. She felt an impulse and, instead of resisting it, she obeyed it.'

The prosecutor stood then and, to underline the serious-
ness of her question, lowered her voice by two tones. It was
her moment, and she knew it. A lot hung in the balance with
this witness.

'Is it possible for a patient's history to predict postpartum
psychosis?'

'It's certainly a factor to take into account.'

'For example?'

'If we know in advance that a patient suffers from bipolar
disorder, that carries a high risk of postpartum psychosis.'

'And what does Mrs Espanet's psychiatric history tell us?
Did she have a history of bipolar disorder?'

'She did not.'

'She had no history of bipolar disorder?'

'No, she had no previous psychiatric record.'

'So Mrs Espanet's mental health was good before the
murders?'

'No, that's not what I said, not at all. But she never ... she
wasn't in the system.'

'Because nothing suggested that she had problems?'

'No, no, no. It's one thing for a person to have never
sought psychiatric help and quite another to say that they ...
When she talks about her past, the patient herself says she
often suffered from depression and bulimia.'

'That's what she says, but there's no diagnosis to back that up.'

'No, but those disorders are consistent with my assess-
ments over the past year.'

'Just to clarify the situation here, doctor: you based your
diagnosis of Alice's psychosis on her behaviour and on her
own account of the events in question, is that correct?'

The prosecutor rolled out this last question very slowly, savouring her victory, knowing that the answer was contained in the question.

But the Belgian psychiatrist responded with the same tone and rhythm.

'What else is there? What else would you need?'

To the disappointment of the prosecutor, most of the jurors nodded instinctively, satisfied.

She thanked the psychiatrist and allowed him to step down.

But the prosecution had no intention of accepting this diagnosis without a fight. Two specialists were called to testify next, the psychiatrists who had treated Alice on the orders of the examining magistrate, after *the act*.

They took the stand to respond, to throw the ball back in the first psychiatrist's court. They had found no signs of psychosis in Alice, nor of postpartum depression. Psychosis, and its results, occurs in the weeks immediately following childbirth, not ten months later. That fact alone was enough to raise doubts.

They told us about several cases, all recent, to give us an idea.

A five-week-old baby in a small town in Toledo, stabbed with a knife.

A mother in Girona, who threw herself out the window holding her 3-month-old.

In Madrid, a baby ten days old, also drowned in the tub.

And so on.

'These cases don't shed any light on the present case; could you explain the connection, please?' Basaguren was quick to respond.

And so they did. In a very clinical manner. And that was where they went wrong. Dryly, as if reading a grocery list, they explained the Beck Depression Inventory and the Edinburgh Postnatal Depression Scale. After this barrage of information, in a truly clumsy move, they read a list of Alice's psychological characteristics with their noses in their notes: narcissism, histrionic tendencies that prevent her from behaving normally in various life situations, self-aggrandisement, low empathy, a tendency to idealise a few people and disregard the rest.

By then, they had lost the jury's attention. One juror was wondering on what weekend the clocks would change, another was considering becoming a vegan once the trial was over, and a third had suddenly begun to notice Carmela Basaguren's low-key sex appeal.

In any case, few were paying attention when one of the experts at last went off script and spoke spontaneously:

'Rather than a disorder, we could say that this is just how she is. Like most of us, she is capable of doing evil but, unlike most of us, she's quite happy to live with that.'

I CALLED MY MOTHER THAT NIGHT.

We normally follow an absurd choreography during telephone calls. If I call her, I prefer it if she doesn't answer; I'd rather leave the ball in her court. That way, when she returns the call, I can decide whether to answer, not answer, or answer only to say, proudly, that I'm very busy and we'll have to talk another time.

But this time that's not what I'm after, I genuinely need to hear her voice.

It bothers me how difficult it is for her to ask about Erik. She usually does it only at the end of our conversations, and solely as a duty, and then she asks me to send pictures. I know she has no real interest, but I send them to her anyway, lots of photos with different poses and different clothes, perhaps one with the striped jumper she gave him, and I feel like an idiot trying to imagine how many seconds she'll devote to each one.

But today I don't want to talk about Erik. I want to talk to her about anything else. Her most recent boyfriend, tantric sex or her various theories about money.

Only when she's talking about things that don't have to do with motherhood does my mother have charisma and light. Only then is she loveable. Otherwise, she isn't. If I bring up things that have to do with motherhood, if I lead her into that dangerous ground, then she becomes grey and dull. And the memories start to flood back, memories that have come to make sense to me only with time: my mother's boredom when she helped me pick up my toys; her disgusted grimace when she wiped my snot; her sour, strained, exhausted expression when my father returned me to *her* house – the house I wanted to consider *ours*; her blank stare as we walked up and down the aisles at the supermarket with me always asking for something, *these biscuits, Mum, multicoloured macaroni, Mum*; and she was deaf and dumb, blind, drowning in her despair, completely isolated.

She answers on the second ring.

How am I, she's fine, just home from her pranayama class. I tell her I'm writing, my new novel is going well, it's a true-crime novel, a legal thriller. She takes my word for it, since she doesn't care much about my writing. I suspect she only skimmed my previous novel, she hardly said anything to me about it.

'How are things going with Niclas?' she asks. 'Are you still connecting in bed?'

I don't know why my mother thinks we ever connected in bed. She's got some nerve asking. Seriously, Mother, don't you remember what it was like to have a small child in the house? No, she doesn't remember. I clarify: 'We don't have a sex life so much as a sex anecdote.'

'Better times will come,' she says. 'Why don't you come here for Christmas and leave the baby with your father?' She can sign us up for a seminar on erotic growth, if we want.

Sometimes I think she must be joking, but no, she is always serious. When I was eighteen, my mother announced that she was leaving. I thought then that she was joking, but she wasn't. She let me keep the flat as long as I was a student, and even until I got a job. But she went to Lanzarote. It was true: she left to live in a meditation retreat centre, to work there and 'grow as a person'. I was already a grown-up, having just turned eighteen. I didn't need my mother, and my father lived nearby, in any case, for emergencies, but I wouldn't need him either. What for? I was eighteen.

I never forgave her, but if I could go back now, I wouldn't know what to do with her.

I ask her for the dates of the seminar on erotic growth, and we hang up politely.

IT SOON BECAME CLEAR THAT THE FORENSIC EVIDENCE WAS of little interest; it added nothing whatsoever to the story. It clarified the crime, in all its simplicity, but not the demon-spirit, in all its atrocity. The security cameras at the house left no room for doubt: no one else was in the house at the time of the children's murders. The autopsy confirmed that the children had drowned in the bath, and water samples from their lungs matched the sample from the bathtub. The job couldn't have been easier for the forensics team.

Nevertheless, a certain diligence was required, as much hung in the balance. And I, believing that the devil is in the details, absorbed all the evidence and explanations with great interest. Police officers from the New Technologies department showed us photos from Alice's phone and computer. Some had already been leaked to the press, and elicited no particular response. They were of the children in conventional clothes, chubby and not especially beautiful, but well cared for in any case, perhaps even loved. There were thousands of photos. Some she had taken on her phone, others were from professional studios. The boy was all smiles, the girl was more serious. And the parents were always the epitome of happiness.

We saw the tub, as of course we had to: made of green plastic, with a cartoon seal with a moustache on one side. The assistant had put it on a wheeled cart and pushed it around the chamber, showing it first to the forensic police, then to all the members of the jury, up close. It was quite an odd moment, tragicomic: the seal, the assistant's plastic gloves, the jury's interest, and the shadow of the dead children, which made us all feel a little guilty.

Worse was the testimony of the forensic doctors, two dark men. They brought photographs. They spoke for too long. And in the end, they only confirmed what all of us already knew. My distress made it impossible to take notes, so I have nothing more to say about it.

THEY WERE CALLED ALEX AND ANGELA, APPROPRIATELY international names for children whose futures would have held German summer camps, Swiss boarding schools and universities in the United Kingdom or the United States. Alex and Angela. I had not known that piece of information until the prosecutor said their names in the first session of the trial. Moreover, I hadn't felt the need for those names until then. They were son and daughter, children, twins, offspring, test-tube siblings, victims, bodies, dust. It was better like that. Everything was worse when you knew their names.

Alex and Angela, with a Basque paternal surname and a French maternal surname. Born one year, dead the next.

Only the prosecutor mentioned their names, and not often. After all, they were just kids.

I SPENT MY AFTERNOONS IN THE PARK. THOUGH I WAS surrounded by mothers, I didn't feel like talking to anyone. If it was raining, there was a café that had a corner full of toys so that kids could play there while their mothers sipped their coffee. Whether I was at the park or in the café, my mind was always far away, at the trial, at the chalet in Armentia, at the tidy but cheap bistro in Bordeaux where it all began.

At night, once Erik was asleep, I used Niclas as a table, as a handball court, as an innocent soul. I tried to write on him, to bounce ideas off him, to corrupt his kind disposition, even just a little.

'What do you think?'

'She must have been ill, what else?'

And if I kept asking, writing, bouncing, corrupting:

'Can't we talk about something else?'

But no, we couldn't, and not because of the trial. We had long since run out of things to talk about, other than our child-rearing project. Once we reported to each other – today he pooped in the tub, today he coughed up so much phlegm, he threw up his whole dinner – we were left empty-handed, and I had nothing but the trial to bring to the table. Did couples really survive beyond raising children? And, if so, how did they manage it?

'The babies were named Alex and Angela, did you know that?'

'No. How would I know a thing like that?'

The quarrel wouldn't last long. Then I would retire to my laptop, leaving Niclas glued to the latest television series. I would open the file of my novel just to make sure it hadn't expanded by itself. Then I would type in my notes for the day. I wanted the trial to end; I thought I had enough material. This theatrical show of a trial was frankly not adding much to the well-rounded story that had been growing inside me for a year and a half. On the contrary, it only added too many grey areas and swamped my neatly-structured project.

It was on one of those days that, like magic, Erik slept for ten hours in a row. Then, two days later, it happened again, and again a little later. It was like the first snow of winter: a silent and hidden event, discreet and elegant. When I opened my eyes in the morning, I felt surprised, and everything around me looked beautiful. By then, I was breastfeeding him only once a day, at night before bed.

IT HAD BEEN PLANNED, OF COURSE. SHE CHOSE A THURSDAY afternoon, when the nanny wasn't there. Her husband was also out. She gave them a pear, half each, mashed with a fork. Then the bottle. It was their last snack, as confirmed by the autopsy. She undressed them. She put one of them down on the floor (the boy?) while she drowned the other. It took only a minute. She laid the dead child (the girl?) on the bed, and took the second in her arms. By then she was an expert at drowning children. Alice never said which order she drowned them in, and the autopsy confirmed only that they had both died at around the same time.

What does it matter whether it was ego-*syntonic* or ego-*dystonic* thoughts that won out in the end? Who cares about Beck or Edinburgh lists? They're only words. Black marks on white paper.

I DID NOT ALWAYS WATCH MADE-FOR-TV FILMS AND CHEAP films on my father's couch. Sometimes there was a programming miracle, and they put on one of those films that stops the world, while my father continued to snore next to me.

Marcello Mastroianni comes to mind, hose in hand, talking with Jack Lemmon in the twilight of their lives.

Death is nothing, says the Italian to the other man, perhaps it erases what a man has done? His achievements, his legacy? But it does not. Death, what are you then? You are nothing. You would like to be as important as life, but life lasts a whole lifetime and you, my friend, last but an instant, the moment you arrive and nothing more.

And there I sit, green Pilot pen and notebook in hand, trying to capture that shining truth tossed out to me by the television. The truths I wrote down in my notebook in my early teens were so dark. ...

And here I sit now, a different notebook in hand, in a trial, thinking, realising that what *caro* Marcello said is not always true. When a small child dies, when he is killed, murdered by a family member, it is his death that is important, not his life. It is his death that remains suspended in space-time, death is his only legacy, not life. His death is what will be remembered, if anything, not his life. Because his life never had a chance. His death was the only star in his night sky.

AND ANOTHER ITALIAN FILM THAT I SAW WHEN I WAS AT THE university. *Roma, città aperta*. Roberto Rossellini's masterwork that gave rise to neorealism. At the end of the film, the Nazis are going to shoot Don Pietro. He helped the partisans, he's a hero like the other partisans, all heroes, all tortured to death without saying a word, without betraying their companions. Another priest tries to console Don Pietro. But Don Pietro is calm, he faces his imminent death with dignity. 'It is not difficult to die well,' he says, in what will be the final dialogue of the film, 'the most difficult thing is to live a good life'. They shoot him, and then a Nazi officer shoots him again in the head, just to be sure.

A good life, dedicated to a good cause. When death makes sense.

The flip side of this can be found in Bertolucci's long film *Novecento*, in the character of histrionic fascist Attila Mellanchini, played by Donald Sutherland. When he's with his lover, a boy approaches: Patrizio, an ardent fan. At first, they include the child in their sex play. But then they get bored and don't need him anymore. Attila picks the child up by the legs and starts laughing and spinning him around, beating the boy's head against the wall over and over, again and again. Until there's barely any head left.

A short life. A harrowing death. One that makes no sense at all.

THEIR NAMES WERE ALEX AND ANGELA. ANGELA AND ALEX. IF they had been given a little more time, they might have become something in life: acrobats, dentists, fans of high-heeled shoes, members of the socialist party, makers of social documentaries, museum managers, professional slackers, oboe players, high-flying artists, high-profile ski instructors, Euro-parliamentarians, climate change deniers, black sheep in a white family. With a little more time, they could have adopted all sorts of habits: living with cocaine addiction, defrauding the public treasury, reading their horoscope every day, talking to strangers in bars, worshipping one god or another, making hand-made Italian pasta, dancing naked in front of the mirror, hating their mother and admiring their father. Clumsy lovers, porn lovers, loners, partiers, de-pressives, optimists, workers, altruists, people who are clean in their habits, who run everywhere, who have to make a real effort to get out of bed, people who love life, are suicidal, are gamblers, are loved, live off someone else, are parents of large families, grandparents of a pack of noisy grand-children.

There is no way of knowing.

3

JUXTA CRUCEM LACRIMOSA

What is the wound of childbirth?
Roasted apple and red wine.
ANONYMOUS, FUNERAL SONG OF MILIA OF LASTUR
(15TH CENTURY)

ONE EVENING, ALICE DREAMED THAT HER CAESAREAN SCAR opened up. Something was scratching her from the inside, a tickle that gradually became a burning sensation, and then there was a great pain and she saw that the wound was widening, the recently-sewn viscous flesh peeling back anew, dripping blood. She tried to close the wound with her hands, but in vain. The flesh had a will of its own, it was a volcano, a cataclysm that would bring about the end of the world. The worst was yet to come, when the flow of blood eased: out of the hot pulp there emerged the leg of a spider, sniffing, groping, a long, hairy spider leg, and then another leg, and another ... until she had to stop looking, drowning in her own screams.

It was no dream.

That is, they wanted to believe that it was a dream, but Alice was awake, just out of the shower, about to put on her nightgown, the rosehip oil she put on her scar still in her hand. And she screamed, and clutched her belly in desperation.

Ritxi gave her a light tranquilliser and put her to bed. That's how he described it in court. He told himself, told his wife, it was just a dream. The nanny also heard the screams, and said so in her testimony. She didn't want to think anything of it, and just let it pass, as she let everything else pass.

I HAD A DREAM THAT NIGHT TOO, I SWEAR.

And Alice was in it, again.

The dream was very simple: the woman was laughing in my face, too close to my face. I punched her right in the face, and her nose crumpled as easily as if it were an empty yoghurt pot.

I didn't hit her again; I gave up because I couldn't hurt her.

THE DEFENCE THOUGHT IT WOULD BE APPROPRIATE TO recount the details of Alice's labour. For that purpose, Carmela Basaguren called a gynaecologist and a midwife as witnesses and, as an expert, a perinatal psychiatrist, who explained the complexities of the neurobiology of childbirth and the latest advances in attachment theory. Another seminar.

Alice gave birth by planned caesarean early in her 37th week because one of the babies – the girl – was breach instead of head down in the birth canal, and there was too little amniotic fluid. At the appointed time, she undressed and was anaesthetised, and the two babies were taken out in the blink of an eye. Then they separated them: Alice went to the recovery room – her blood pressure had dropped – where she trembled for two hours, crying and unable to move her hands because of the anaesthesia. She felt a terrible thirst but was not allowed to drink any water. Ritxi was given cotton swabs with lemon juice and tried to freshen his wife's mouth with them for an hour. The babies had disappeared and they didn't know how they were doing, but Alice had no strength to ask after them. She was still trembling and still couldn't move her hands, which were folded across her chest. She felt nauseous. The boy had been placed in an incubator with low birth weight, hypoglycemia, low platelet count and respiratory distress. The girl spent the whole day in the NICU as a precaution; she was fine.

According to the psychiatrist, the effect of those first difficult hours should not be underestimated. For one thing, a planned caesarean bypassed the fundamental neuro-biological process of childbirth, most importantly, the healing flow of oxytocin. Furthermore, the chance to bond was lost. This could have long-term effects: the mother could experience intense alienation from the child, with lifelong consequences for the baby.

Remembering the first time I was apart from Erik, I took the psychiatrist for an alarmist. My own birth went well, and my mother kept me continually by her side, yet this did not prevent her early alienation, nor, no doubt, the long-lasting consequences for me.

In any case, the psychiatrist spoke with great enthusiasm. She was scientific, but also informative, and what she said was both believable and based on data obtained through serious research. It was clear that the jurors loved her.

Furthermore, the separation had made breastfeeding difficult. Without the stimulation of the babies, Alice never produced enough milk. A midwife visited her room every morning and squeezed Alice's nipples, sometimes with a hellish machine, sometimes by hand. On the third day, just when they thought her milk was about to come in, Alice tearfully told the midwife not to come back. She could not bear to have her nipples so cruelly pinched any more, nor did she want to see the midwife's disappointment, all for four miserable drops of milk. The babies would be just fine on powdered milk. She knew there was a pill for women in her situation. Where could she get it?

THIS IS HOW A CAESAREAN IS DONE.

The woman is anaesthetised, normally from the chest down, and is conscious the whole time. She is positioned with her arms apart and her wrists tied. She's given a drip and her vital signs are monitored. A tube is inserted into her urethra so that her bladder will be empty, and another goes in her nose to provide complementary oxygen.

Her abdomen and upper pubic area are shaved. The skin is disinfected.

Then the doctor asks for the scalpel.

The first cut: laparotomy. A transverse incision about fifteen centimetres long in the lower abdomen. (The transverse incision is an innovation in the history of the caesareans, and it has one clear advantage: a bikini will hide the scar).

After the first incision, the fat layer is retracted and the firm tissue that connects to the muscles (the aponeurosis) is cut horizontally, usually with surgical scissors. Next, the abdominal muscles are pulled apart by hand and the peritoneum, the thin tissue that contains the internal organs, is opened with the fingers.

After this excavation, the uterus – the treasure chest – can be seen, and it's time for the second cut: hysterotomy, the surgical incision of the uterus. The amniotic sac is ruptured and any remaining amniotic fluid is drained: now the baby can be taken out. After cutting the umbilical cord, the placenta is removed by hand.

Then it's time to suture the incisions, working backwards, one step at a time.

First the uterus. The peritoneum is not stitched, it will heal by itself. The aponeurosis, which supports the muscles, does need sutures. Last is the skin, which is sometimes stapled.

The whole surgery lasts about an hour.

The stitches remain in the skin for a week.

The body absorbs the uterine sutures within forty days.

Abdominal pain may last months.

Other less visible complications may last the rest of the woman's life: injury to the adjacent organs, adhesion between organs, difficulty getting pregnant again, or not being able to at all.

It is not true that Julius Caesar was born by caesarean section. His mother, Aurelia, died aged 66, when her most famous son was 46 and, until the 20th century (with only two or three exceptions) all women who underwent caesarean died, if not by haemorrhage, then from infection a few days later.

WHEN THEY WENT HOME FROM THE HOSPITAL, SOMETHING happened. They were driving home with Angela for the first time; Alex was still in the hospital. Alice sat in the back with the baby. The trip was quite short, only fifteen minutes. Ritxi was nervous, but overflowing with joy. He wanted to make plans, to plan out all the hours to come. Alice, however, seemed downcast, bags under her eyes on her grey and weary face. It must be because she had to leave the other child at the hospital, thought her husband. But he would also be home soon, and they'd visit him at the hospital later that afternoon. Alice met Ritxi's gushing with defiant silence until he fell quiet. He turned on the radio to a classical music station, Fauré's *Requiem*. He was tired too, and had to admit that his joy was largely fabricated. At a red light, with no warning, Alice suddenly undid the baby's seat belt, undid her own seat belt, and got out of the car, carrying the baby. Ritxi froze, not understanding what was going on, and waited for something to occur to him. The light turned green. Ritxi didn't know what to do. He was used to obeying traffic lights, and the cars behind him were honking. Finally, he too got out of the car, and found his wife sheltering in a doorway, singing a lullaby to the baby.

'What are you doing, Alice?'

'We can't stay in that car,' she said calmly. 'The fumes will kill her.'

'What fumes? What are you talking about?'

'The gas fumes.'

It took five minutes to convince her there were no fumes inside the car, that the child was fine, everything was fine. Alice didn't seem nervous, just stubborn, convinced. In the end, Ritxi had to promise her that they'd keep the windows down all the way home, and had to convince two policemen, who had come to investigate the cause of the traffic disturbance, that everything was fine, they were moving on, it had all just been a misunderstanding. Since they had a newborn with them, they let them go without asking too many questions.

They didn't speak again the rest of the way home. The baby started to cry, and Alice spent the whole time trying to calm her down with a dummy, but Angela kept refusing it, or didn't yet have the strength to suck on it. Once they got home, there was so much to do with the baby that they never spoke about what had happened.

But did this not set off any alarms for him? Could he not see a reason to seek some help?

Ritxi, sitting before the microphone, rubbed the space between his eyebrows before answering. He took a ragged breath.

Yes, of course. That was why they had hired Mélanie: to lighten the load. That was why a reiki master came to their house: to relieve his wife's chronic sadness. That was why she went to Pilates twice a week. All of this seemed to help, the situation seemed to be under control.

It wasn't enough? Obviously not. But what could Ritxi do now? What?

(By the way, it came out in the trial that the Gasteiz police have no record of any traffic incident on the day Ritxi spoke of.)

OF ALL THE WITNESSES, THE ONLY ONE TO TESTIFY BEHIND A
screen was Mélanie, the nanny. She had turned down the
assistance of an interpreter, but could not face Alice. This
prop, requested by the nanny, undoubtedly scored a point
for the prosecution as a clear display of the risk, the threat
posed by Alice, her wickedness.

On the other hand, Mélanie's explanations made it clear
that Alice was not quite right in the head. It remained to be
seen to what extent, and how far that might go in explaining
the events.

How long had Mélanie worked for Alice and Ritxi? Since
the babies were one month old, until ... well, until the end.
Had Mélanie enjoyed the job? Not much. Why not? Mélanie
didn't hesitate: because of the children's mother. You never
knew how she was going to behave. Sometimes she was
looking over her shoulder from morning to night, supervising
the children's care. Other times, she dismissed her pleas-
antly, even merrily, and locked herself in her studio, apparently to paint, leaving Mélanie to do all the work. The nanny
preferred the latter, of course, despite the workload. On days
when Alice was right on top of her, her mood was unpredict-
able. She might be bad-tempered, criticising the nanny's
every move, or depressed, discouraged because the babies
weren't gaining enough weight, or they were too fat, or they
weren't sleeping enough, or they were sleeping too much,
whatever could be wrong with them?

Had Mélanie noticed anything else unusual?

Sometimes Alice burst in on Mélanie, upset and distressed, saying the children were 'lost.' At first she would
also get upset and run to the children's room, where they

napped, and where, to her relief, she would find them, right where she had left them five minutes earlier. Alice did this four or five times, until Mélanie resigned herself to calming her down, without paying much attention to her distress. 'They're not lost, Alice, they're in their room, go and see.'

If only she had paid more attention. ...

If only she had talked to the father about the mother's state of mind ... But the father was hardly ever home, and when he did come home, he barely even acknowledged her existence.

If only she hadn't been so quick to go out that Thursday, with that boy she had only just met. ...

But it was her only afternoon off. And the only boy in her new city who had asked her out, frankly.

'In your opinion, did Alice love her children?' asked Carmela Basaguren with apparent sincerity.

'She worried about them a lot. Does that count?'

Mélanie was in tears at the end of her testimony and two jurors also had to wipe their eyes. Again.

But I never once saw Alice cry.

'SHE'S NOT GOING TO GET OFF, YOU KNOW THAT, RIGHT?'

Someone on my left was talking to me. We were standing at the bar, having a coffee and a potato omelette.

'Excuse me?'

'No matter what that French woman's lawyer does, she's going to jail.'

'Oh.'

'Sorry. Since I see you at the trial every day, I thought you would have noticed me too, but I guess not.'

I didn't know what to say, because the truth was I had noticed him, he was a journalist who sat in the front row every day, so dark-skinned he looked Hindu, so slender he looked like a ballet dancer, so handsome that if he ever spoke to me, I would only stutter like an idiot. As I was doing right then, in fact.

'You're not a journalist, are you?'

'No, no, I'm here to do research.'

'Oh, you're from the university!'

I didn't say no, but I also didn't quite feel that my lack of response was a lie.

'When there's no doubt, when the accused was caught *in fraganti* or makes a clear confession ... there's only one card left for the lawyers to play. Insanity. And there will always be a psychiatrist who's willing to play along. Ego-syntonic, ego-whatever, imprinting ... as if we were ducklings. They must be really desperate to start trotting out all that jargon. I'm Jakes, by the way.'

And he mentioned the newspaper he worked for. 'So you're not Hindu?' I was about to ask. Fortunately, I reined myself in, just in time.

'This case is quite unusual, anyway. A mother, her own children ...' I would have said anything to keep the conversation going.

'It happens more often than you think, actually. In fact, we're all more likely to be killed by a family member than by a stranger.'

'There's also her profile,' I added, though I wanted nothing more than to agree with this man in everything he said.

'Ah, yes, exactly. Foreign, rich, full support of her husband ... She's certainly no desperate, lower-class unwed mother!'

'And she's very beautiful.'

'That too. But with this citizen's jury, she hasn't got a chance.'

'Why not?'

'Most of them are women, for one thing. And especially, because juries tend to be cruel. Did you know that, compared to decisions made by judges, juries have a higher conviction rate? Give your average person a little bit of power and they show no mercy!'

Oh, Jakes, why didn't you come over to talk to me on the first day? Why now, on the next-to-the-last day of the trial, when I'm grabbing my hat and coat and leaving this party? You had so many interesting things to share with me! But now that you're in my orbit, I won't let you get away so easily.

'But you personally, what do you think? Why did she do it?' I asked him.

'Because she realised she didn't want children. She didn't love them, they were nothing but a burden to her. She wanted to get rid of that burden, and thought she had every right to do so. And above all else, of course, because she's heartless and unable to love.'

'That simple?'

'Why not? Sometimes that's all it is.'

A father eats dinner with his family: lasagna and yoghurt. Then they all watch television together: a silly competition of some sort. As he does every night, he kisses his 6- and

8-year-old daughters, asleep in their bunk beds. He also gives his wife a kiss on the neck while she smooths her anti-wrinkle cream under her eyes, chatting about what they have to do the next day. Then he goes into his study, takes a pistol out of the drawer and puts it in his mouth. Bang. No note. The pistol is the message.

It happens. That's the true story of the father of one of my classmates. That simple.

There are those who go right up to the edge of the cliff of the soul. In such dire straits, some feel the urge to jump, others feel like shoving the person next to them over the edge. The death drive. The greatest dose of power one can ever experience. The power to end it all. Something that can be done so quickly and effectively that, once done, incredulity eclipses regret.

I wanted to say all this to Jakes, but the words wouldn't come.

'Yes, yes, yes, that's what humans are like, but even so ...'

'Even so, even so. Yeah. Rhetorical tricks like these are for the defence. Shall we go back in? Recess is over,' said Jakes, with an open, childlike smile that made my knees weak.

'Sure, let's go.'

IN ALICE'S BIOGRAPHY, THERE'S A GIANT HOLE THAT NO ONE seems to be interested in filling in. Or that no one can fill in. Thanks to Léa, I know more or less what kind of life Alice led until she was 21 or 22. The trial examined her marriage, her fertility treatment, her complicated motherhood. In between, there was an interval of three or four years in which she dropped off the radar, and during which at least one notable thing happened: she changed her name. She kills off Jade and ushers in Alice. Why?

'Because Jade seemed too lower-class, or to go against her mother,' said Léa, when I asked her about it on Telegram. She didn't seem to think it was very important. Alice had kept her mother's surname, Espanet. Though this too was insignificant, according to my friend.

TWO MONTHS AFTER ALICE AND RITXI MET IN BORDEAUX, Alice was living in Gasteiz. Her weekend visits had become week-long visits and soon, though gradually, all of her things had been moved into Ritxi's penthouse on San Antonio Street. All of her things consisted of a bunch of clothes and make-up, moved to Gasteiz in different phases in small suitcases. Ritxi organised a society dinner at which he would introduce his fiancée to all his friends. His friends don't remember much about the dinner. A young woman, slender and discreet. Pretty much what they had expected. They weren't surprised to receive their invitations to the wedding shortly thereafter. They did the usual. Organised a stag do for Ritxi: a weekend in Ibiza, a sailing boat, a case of Veuve Clicquot. That was as much as they cared to talk about in a trial. They also convinced their wives and girlfriends to organise something for Alice. So, under duress, the flock of females took the mysterious Frenchwoman (they all freely admitted that she was still mysterious) out for brunch at the only hotel in Gasteiz that did such things, then went to a spa in the afternoon for Iong Bao massages. Alice had no close friends amongst the women, but they treated her well enough, according to the woman who acted as the spokesperson for the group at the trial. It was Alice who always kept her distance, Alice who declined to take part in conversation, Alice who answered all their questions with an ironic smile. Without saying it in so many words, she gave them to understand that she had suffered a lot in life and therefore looked down on them, because they had never known true pain, these healthy and elitist women who had lived their lives in comfort and warmth.

These women did not understand – the witness spoke in the plural, underlining the tribal nature of the group – how Alice could be so ungrateful. Though who knows where she had come from? She had been flattered and welcomed into their elite echelon only because, one fine day, a man had set eyes on her and liked what he saw. The witness didn't use those exact words, but that was basically what she meant. And now that Alice knew all the passwords to their privileged world, all she did was turn her nose up at them, and make disparaging comments if one of them mentioned that her new fashion blog was becoming 'so successful', or if another tearfully recounted the dramatic quarrel she'd had with the designer who was remodelling her living room and kitchen.

They barely saw her outside of social commitments. One of the last times had been at a baby shower that they threw for her just before the twins were born. They always held a shower when one of them was pregnant, and saw no way to get out of it in Alice's case. It was held on a rainy day in the chalet in Armentia, and they were all quite shocked to see that Alice was drinking wine (two glasses at least, as far as they knew, and not even from her own husband's cellar!), and noted that she mentioned the mortal dangers of childbirth over and over. Apparently, she had studied the statistics in great detail, and knew that, in the Basque Autonomous Community, 4.7 out of every 1,000 babies died in childbirth, or soon after. She seemed convinced that her twins would not survive the test, and they thought that was why, as soon as she opened the gifts (video baby monitors, an ergonomic backpack, a LED light projection lamp), she set them all aside without showing any emotion at all, utterly indifferent.

No, they didn't like Alice, but deep down they were happy enough to have a reason to gossip and bitch about someone. They certainly couldn't deny that she had brought them many hours of catty entertainment. Alice, always cause for scandal and disbelief, had become the guest star of many private conversations and secret, whispered phone calls.

This last part was obvious to me, though the witness didn't say any of it. I wrote it down in my notebook.

'THAT RICH BITCH CERTAINLY MADE A BAD IMPRESSION,' SAID Jakes after the session, as I was rushing out the door, keys in hand.

'Do you really think so?' I put the keys back in my handbag unconsciously. 'The things she said about Alice didn't make her look too good either.'

'Yes, but who are you going to believe? That plastic Barbie who spends all her time and her husband's money on massages and three thousand-euro handbags, or tragic, deep, mysterious Alice?'

'Well, she didn't exactly choose the best wardrobe for going to a trial. Those heels ...'

'Chanel boots.'

'... For example.'

(Did this man know something about everything?)

'Listen, I'm dying of hunger, shall we go get something to eat? You still haven't told me anything about your research.'

He tossed out the invitation as if it were nothing, and my heart leaped. I reacted quickly, however, following my basest instinct: prudence.

'I can't today. I have to get back to Bilbao.'

I didn't explain why, or who I would be spending the afternoon with.

'That's too bad.'

'Maybe tomorrow?'

'Tomorrow's the last day of the trial.'

'We can celebrate.'

'Okay.'

We shook on it; he must surely have noticed I was trembling.

On the motorway, I started talking to myself out loud, which I only do when I'm either very drunk or very nervous.

'Just what the hell do you think you're doing? Shit, it's a date, right?'

'How could it be a date, you idiot? It'll be like a working lunch, that's all, just to talk about the case. He doesn't know anything about you and you don't know anything about him.

What if he's married?'

'Well, you're married!'

'Exactly. Two married people, there's nothing romantic going on here. Besides, didn't you think it was strange that he knew about Chanel boots?'

'What are you saying? You think he's gay? Your old-fashioned prejudices are showing, girl!'

I only managed to shut up when I rolled my window down at the tollbooth, but my insides were still bubbling away. I hadn't felt like that for a long time, perhaps not since I was fifteen. I had to tread carefully, or there was a high probability I'd do something ridiculous. More than the fact that this attractive man had noticed me, what really made me happy was my own interest in him. Ever since I'd been pregnant, I had felt as if I were in a cave, and it was only now, two years later, that I could see the sun again, stretch, feel my muscles warm and ready themselves for erotic pleasures.

I had a lot of hard work ahead of me.

4
MOTHERS' DREAMS

Why has no one come up with an equivalent of Ikea for childcare, an equivalent of Microsoft for housework?
VIRGINIE DESPENTES, *KING KONG THEORY*

IN KIDS' STORIES, IT'S ALWAYS THE STEPMOTHER WHO'S EVIL, never the mother. It's the stepmother who enslaves Cinderella. The stepmother, again, who wants to have Snow White's heart to keep in a box. The mother never appears in these stories, she's long dead, forgotten. The only escape for these young ladies is to free themselves from their step-mothers. Whence this obsession with stepmothers? Psychoanalysis tells us that the figure of the stepmother is a reflection of the child's dissociation. The mother and the stepmother are really one and the same. One is the shadow of the other. It's not acceptable for the mother to be devious, or cruel, so she becomes the stepmother; she is the other, no longer the mother. Until she returns to kindness and tender-ness, she can't win back the title of mother.

This is not a psychological need only of children.

Judeo-Christian tradition takes this dissociation to absurd lengths, going as far as to have invented the figure of the virgin mother. The virgin mother (?). The virgin mother is not a true Judeo-Christian invention. It's another mytheme.

A cyclical and interchangeable narrative element that crops up here and there in civilizations that have never had any direct contact with each other. Athena, one of the most important goddesses in Greek mythology, goddess of wisdom and war, was a virgin. Hephaestus desired her, so much that he ejaculated over her clothes. Athena, disgusted, flung his seed to the ground, where suddenly a son was born, Erichthonius, whom Athena took as her son, maintaining her virginity, of course. Maya, mother of the Buddha, was impregnated by a ray of light (Buddha means 'enlightened,' after all) after the coming miracle had been revealed to her in a dream. Coatlicue, goddess of Aztec mythology, was impregnated while she was sweeping a temple and a ball of feathers fell from the heavens and touched her skin; this led to the birth – a pure birth – of Huitzilopochtli. Persian god Mithra was born from the guts of Anahita, but in a quite unusual way (or usual), since Anahita was a virgin.

Whence this recurring obsession with virgin pregnancy?

It is hysterical, anti-biological, anti-empirical dissociation.

Not to mention misogynistic.

If a woman is a mother, there can be no sex involved. Once she falls into the clutches of sex, she is a whore. If she is a whore, she cannot give life, on the contrary, she is dangerous and may easily become a killer, taking the life of any and all who get too close. If she's not a killer, not a whore … that's the mother, giver of life.

Or, to put it more simply:

All whores, except my mother.

We've heard that song before, many times.

However, Carmela Basaguren was skilled at telling new stories, certainly more skilled than the prosecution. The public prosecutor had entered the fray believing that this would be an open-and-shut case, but now found herself entangled in the biblical contradictions of a murderous mother, and swamped in psychiatric jargon that explained nothing. I saw the prosecutor discreetly wipe the sweat from her brow more than once when the defence attacked her with everything they had: psychosis, insanity, hallucinations, what else could it be, can't you see, how else could you explain this.

However, I thought the shadows of the two children must be there, someone must be thinking about them, someone would be thinking about what a cruel end they had come to, lungs filling with water, faces turning blue. At their own mother's hands. Those hands that decided to keep going. Or were the prosecutor and I the only ones who wanted to hold onto the fine thread of the children's memory?

THE EVIL MOTHER VS. THE GOOD WRITER: ANOTHER dissociation.

An unfinished checklist:

- The good writer locks herself in her room and does not open the door, even if her child pounds on it. Even if her child starts begging and crying, the good writer stands firm. She will use earplugs. She will put another lock on the door. She is writing.

- The good writer hires nannies to be with the children while she is writing.
- The good writer uses her own motherhood as material for her literature, even though, while she is writing, she cannot act as a mother.
- The good writer reads books about attachment theory, about the physiology of childbirth, and about child-rearing methods in Ancient Greece. Because she has her nose in a book, she doesn't see that her child has fallen off the slide.
- The good writer, holding her pup in her arms for the first time in the birthing room, is already thinking about how to describe this experience in an original way.
- The good writer can comment on Madame Bovary from a gender perspective, explaining why her sexual desire and lack of maternal instinct are one and the same thing, and must be the same thing.
- The good writer has sometimes gone so far as to envy Emma Bovary, who left her daughter in the care of a wet nurse, and saw her only on Sundays (some Sundays, a few Sundays).
- The good writer wonders if her children will ever forgive her for being such a good writer.

- The good writer would actually like to be
  a man.

THE ATOM, THE GRAIN OF SAND. THEY SAY THE WHOLE universe is contained in them. Just as each of our tiny movements can precipitate the most definitive movement. The brief but eternal movement that turns life into death. Seen only by those with a cyclical understanding of time.

Alice never completely abandoned her passion for painting. Her hands were always dirty. In the house in Armentia, she had her own studio for exactly this purpose. Ritxi had always liked his wife's hobby, and had encouraged her to keep doing it. Alice went to her studio every day. Sometimes she produced something. During the year of the events in question, she had given up watercolours and started using oil paints, experimenting with collage. She continued to paint the female body, bodies that were more and more deformed, blood here and there, menstrual blood, the blood of childbirth, a pain that was always visible, in red.

'Why don't you paint the spider?' Ritxi asked.

So Alice did. She splashed her caesarean across the canvas, the wound opening, the hairy legs of the spider. The paintings got bigger and bigger. She glued red plastic onto them here and there. She used wire for the spider's legs, wire that tore at her belly. She cut the hair off all the stuffed animals they had in the house to stick it on her paintings. Those hairy animals had already lost their spider shape in splashes of blood.

Ritxi was truly impressed. He didn't know much about art, but apparently his own sensibility was sufficient for him to judge whether or not what he was seeing was any good. He had nine powerful paintings in front of him, no doubt about it.

'We need to have an exhibition.'

'I don't have time, the kids ...' said Alice quickly, as if she had already thought about it.

'The kids are fine. We have Mélanie, and I'll help you too.'

She gave in; Alice had given in quickly since the day she gave birth.

They would have it at Ritxi's winery, in the elegant room where the visitors had their tastings. They would hold an opening party, he knew which friends to invite, he would choose the right ones. A small catalogue would have to be designed, his publicity girl could run one up in no time. The paintings would be for sale, of course, from €180 to €300, depending on their size. And Ritxi had more plans in mind. He felt that he had suddenly come up with a solution to his wife's chronic sadness, and his thoughts were racing: Alice would design a label with the same motifs as her paintings, though without the emotional rawness, of course, to make it more commercial, but those spiders would be perfect for the labels of a signature wine he had been thinking about for ages. He would call the wine *Alice*, obviously.

On the opening day of the exhibition, Ritxi and Alice headed for La Rioja before noon, leaving the twins with Mélanie. Alice never went to her husband's workplace. She was nervous, but also excited. Her first exhibition. And it was also the first time she had been away from the babies for such a long time. Almost a whole day, at least eight or nine hours. She called Mélanie every half an hour. The nanny answered only about half the time. She was fed up, and finally told Alice she was busy changing nappies and feeding the kids fruit, she couldn't be answering the phone all the time as well.

Everything was ready by the time they arrived. The employees at the winery had hung the nine paintings, chosen the wine that would be served, set everything out on tall tables, and were managing the catering. The publicity girl had the catalogue ready, a simple triptych printed on standard size paper and folded by hand. Eighty copies were fanned out on the table in the middle of the room.

Alice was left hanging. Everything was ready by the time she arrived, and now she had nothing to do but wait. Ritxi got caught up in work (a phone call), and then another issue (a supposedly quick meeting with the marketing woman), even though he'd promised her he wouldn't work that day, he would devote the whole day to Alice's exhibition.

'Why don't you go for a walk, love? Now that it's stopped raining.'

The mid-spring day was cold and unpleasant. The grapevines looked like charred stumps. Alice rarely went to La Rioja, and now she remembered why. She didn't like the landscape, not even at its peak in the autumn; the colour palette was exhausting. She preferred cooler shades.

Ritxi had renovated the winery himself after his father's death. To the hundred-year-old building he'd added a great dome of glass that now served as its entrance. Alice decided to walk around the old building. If she strayed too far, her shoes would get muddy and she hadn't brought another pair with her. She was having doubts about the outfit she had chosen. Black, from top to toe. If only she had brought a colourful scarf instead of this grey rag. Her head started to pound, and she had to stop her reluctant walk. She leaned against the wall and lit a cigarette. She shivered, and then she heard the words that slipped out through a window that was cracked open:

'A cheap copy of Louise Bourgeois, and the same thing nine times over besides. But whatever. They'll all be sold in the first half an hour, since everyone wants to get in Ritxi's good graces. And to think I had to spend an hour making an "art catalogue"...'

It was the publicity girl, talking with someone on her phone. Alice tossed her cigarette to the ground and stamped it out with her black shoes.

Ritxi found his wife half an hour later. She was in the tasting room, with the paintings. But there were no paintings there any more, or at least not whole ones. Alice had taken one of the bottles of wine reserved for the opening and smashed it against a table. With the broken neck of the bottle, she was slashing the paintings, one by one, methodically, sometimes with such violence that she shattered the wooden frame as well. The wine, splashed over the floor and walls, gave the destruction an undeniable touch of gore.

'The exhibition is over,' said Alice. 'Let's go home. I want to see the kids.'

She wrapped her scarf around her neck and got ready to go. Ritxi asked her to wait for him in the car, he would have to talk to his employees before he left, and somehow explain what had happened.

But Ritxi did not seek help, even after this episode. He tried to explain why he hadn't at the trial, since the prosecutor thought this all very strange, all the more so when the publicity girl showed the photos she had taken, without asking anyone, of the post-apocalyptic scene at the exhibition. There was great rage behind this artistic massacre. Why hadn't her husband done anything?

Ritxi calmly explained his side of the story. Was what had happened all that strange, after all? He didn't think so. And he gave his reasons:

1) The pathological dissatisfaction of the artist (he reminded us that Kafka had asked a friend to burn all his writings).

2) The lack of confidence of anyone who presents such intimate work to the public (he was no artist, but he could understand that sudden insecurity).

3) Jealousy, perhaps (here he made reference to certain physical characteristics of the publicity girl, subtly but clearly). And finally,

4) Despite the seemingly dire consequences, everything had been cleaned up (by other people) in the blink of an eye, with no more than a mop and a cleaning cloth. It was a studied explanation, delivered carefully, and Ritxi practically shrugged on the stand, as if to say there was no relationship between the aborted exhibition and *the act*, as if talking about all this were nothing but a waste of time.

Perhaps he was right.

Who knows?

What would I know?

Perhaps it's not true that the essence of the whole universe is contained in a single atom. The grain of sand may be no more than a grain of sand. And the most definitive movement may happen without warning. No one can predict which kernel of corn in the pan will pop first.

ANOTHER GAP. PERHAPS DUE TO THE LACK OF A SPECIFIC accusation. We hardly know anything about Alice's life after the events. What little we know comes from intriguing sources: her husband, and the Belgian psychiatrist who's been treating her for the last year. Both talked about withdrawal and isolation. Alice barely leaves the house. She takes strong medication. She's never alone, she's under the care of a nurse when Ritxi is at work. She often goes to Barcelona to see the Belgian psychiatrist. From the car to the plane, from the plane to the taxi, from the taxi to the psychiatrist's office, and back, all on the same day. Ritxi gives her everything: all his time, his money, his love. The last of these seems to be limitless. He's lost his children, he at least wants his wife back, the love of his life. The psychiatrist says she's getting better. But she'll need time. More therapy, lots of pills. And the probability of relapse will always be high. No, under no circumstances could he recommend that she have more children.

But there's no way of knowing if they're telling the truth. Whatever Alice does inside her house is a mystery. If she emerges, and what she does when she emerges: there's no way of knowing.

In other cases, with greater means, a private detective would follow the accused for weeks, months. Studying her behaviour, documenting everything, catching her out in her lies.

But no one has taken on this task. There is no specific accusation that protects the interests of the children. After all, they were only children and no one even remembers them much anymore.

I'VE ALREADY MENTIONED THE TWO MAIN FEELINGS I HAD during Erik's first months: boredom and exhaustion. I have yet to mention a third even though it was easily as significant as the others: fear. Why didn't I mention it? Because it's almost embarrassing. The other two emotions make me seem like an independent woman, while fear turns me into just an ordinary woman destined for Biblical suffering. Yet the fear was there. Almost continually, like background music. Like a sweaty dance partner who won't let go of you. Fear.

It's a terrible thing to have a vivid imagination. Well, it can be good for sexual fantasies, and in a couple of other areas in life, perhaps. But most of the time, it's a curse. Who could rein in the deranged imagination of a mother? My fear was very specific, but its branches were twisted and endless. The many ways Erik could die swarmed inside me.

For example:

He could fall into the stream while I was pushing him in the pushchair, crossing a bridge. A nudge from a passing jogger, a careless stumble would be enough. Would I be able to hurl myself into the water to save him? I didn't think so, the weight of the pushchair would sink my baby too fast.

Another fear, one that makes me blush now, but at the time, one I saw as a real possibility:

I would accidentally put Erik in the washing machine. Why not? It was possible. The baby would be sleeping on a blanket in a corner of the living room, and I, in my sleepdeprived fog, would be picking up the dirty clothes from the floor, automatically, towels with spit-up on them, baby blankets, and in amongst the jumble, I would pick up his small body too, without noticing, he weighed so little, and load him into the machine without hearing his cries. Only after I pushed the button for the quick cycle would I realise what I had done. The laundry would start turning, the drum would fill with water in just a few seconds. The washing machine can't be opened when it's full of water. As if on a screen, I would watch my baby's agonising death. A fleeting shiver of panic would run up my spine every time I pushed the button on the machine.

There was more: open windows, toys that could get stuck in his throat, plug sockets, bottles of bleach, the cord of an iron, hot oil that could splash out of the frying pan, and many more things suggested by the flyer the Health Service handed out, they were all out there, always, always, always. Lurking.

There was no rest to be had.

It seemed to me that the child's natural destiny was to be the victim of an accident. And it was very clear to me that, if someone wanted to kill a child, a bit of *laissez-faire* would be sufficient: a few marbles among his toys, his chair next to an open window, a box of washing powder under the kitchen table. It was just a matter of time.

Just sit and wait for it to happen.

The perfect crime.

Alice's problem, of course, was that instead of one, she had two. Two such accidents were beyond all laws of probability.

WE HAVE ONE OF LOUISE BOURGEOIS' SPIDERS IN BILBAO, IN a wing of the Guggenheim Museum. The sculpture is called *Maman*. I've passed under those long legs more than once on my walks with Erik. If you stop beneath the animal and look up, you can see eggs in a sac between its legs. It's a mother. Like me. Because for Bourgeois, the spider represents the protective web of motherhood.

'Spiders make pleasant company. They eat mosquitoes. They're proactive and they're always helpful. That's what my mother was like,' said the Parisian artist in an interview.

Bourgeois' spiders, therefore, are not repugnant creatures that pierce the uterus and push their way through, layer by layer, until they reach the surface, covered in blood.

THE LAST DAY OF THE TRIAL. AFTER THIS SESSION, THE JURY will retire to deliberate for a day, two days, who knows.

The final hurdle. Sit on the usual bench with the innocence of law students, who have clear, legitimate, understandable pedagogical intentions.

A journey of almost three weeks was coming to an end. Unlike Hollywood films, this had been a theatrical work full of long, insignificant, boring statements. There might still have been a climax, however, if Alice had entered a final plea, and that's what I was waiting for.

But, especially ...

That was the day I was supposed to have lunch with Jakes. That's why I put lipstick on for the final session, of course. That's why I was trembling, that's mostly why. Would he remember our date? Or would I have to remind him, seemingly indifferent? Still want to have lunch, Jakes? You'll have to decide where, I don't know this area very well.

I didn't know if I'd be able to. But I would have to be. I had told Niclas that this last session would be longer than usual, he was happy that the trial was almost over and didn't ask too many questions. On top of that, as an anomaly, and at the last minute, I had asked my father to pick Erik up from the nursery. It was a beautiful sunny autumn day, they could spend a couple of hours in the park until I arrived, with a bit of luck he wouldn't even have to change Erik's nappy during that time. The web of logistics and lies was too complicated now for my dark-haired date to stand me up. But, on the other hand, if the date didn't happen, surely I would feel the relief of one who has escaped a large and sticky spider's web. I'm such a coward sometimes.

What were my intentions towards Jakes? Truly, just lunch. A short, mild flirtation. A few coquettish laughs, and some fodder for future fantasies. Nothing more. Frivolous conversation at first, then, when choosing the wine, I would let it drop that I knew a little something about it, I would mention that I had lived in London for a few years (the card I always play when I sense that interest in me is waning) and, once the second course arrived, we'd get down to business: we'd talk about the case, I would reveal at last that I was a writer ('Of course! I thought I recognised your face!' said this

handsome man in my wildest fantasy, 'I loved your novel!'),
writing about Alice's crime, and that I had to understand
why she did it, why the hell she did what she did.

Erotic longing and intellectual longing were one and the
same, then. Many things would become clear while talking
with Jakes. I needed someone who was as well-versed in the
case as I was, but that wasn't me. That's how the book would
move forward, that's how it would take the shape I imagined
it could have. I placed all my hopes in Jakes now. I had no
Plan B. The dark-haired man I had met the day before held
all the keys. At that moment, the idea made sense and put
me in a good mood. I couldn't even discount the idea of
making Jakes a character and introducing him towards the
end of the book.

And that was it. No more, no less. At most, we'd share our
desserts. He'd eat some of my brownie, I'd try some of his
crème caramel. At most, when I got home in the evening, I'd
write Léa a message mentioning what I'd almost done.

'*Bitch!*' she would say, 'You whore, look at you, you should
know better. I stopped all that long ago, as you well know.
Danger! Danger!'

It was no small thing.

So, the last session. Perhaps Alice would go straight to jail
from the trial, perhaps for the rest of her life. On the motorway again, for the last time. The motorway, the court, my
notebook full of notes, and then, at last, I would write without
a safety net. Start writing, once and for all. With the confidence, the blind faith, that a story would come out of this.
I was sacrificing too much, and that could only mean a
masterwork would flow from my fingertips. Of course it

would, I would rise to the challenge. All would be revealed through writing, all would be allowed. The furious rhythm of the keys would bare the truth. And I would understand it. And everyone would understand why I did what I did.

With Jakes' help.

Tally of the sacrifices of the mother and writer. Another unfinished checklist:

√ The couple relationship, including its inner honesty, network of trust and treasure trove of intimacy. SACRIFICED.

√ Valuable hours of quality time, essential for the emotional development of my son. SACRIFICED.

√ Economic stability (current state of my bank account, with the book still unwritten: €2,897). SACRIFICED.

√ Privilege of considering myself a good person. Or in other words, the privilege of not feeling like an obscene vulture circling above two murdered children. SACRIFICED.

THE PROSECUTOR BEGAN HER CLOSING ARGUMENT BY mentioning the children's names.

'They were called Alex and Angela, in case anyone's forgotten. They were people like us, with their whole lives ahead of them, they needed someone who would love them and take care of them, they were both unique and wonderful, just like each of us.'

A pause, and the judge's heavy breathing, suddenly audible.

'But the world, alas, the world is not always the way we're told it is. Mothers are not always the way we're told they are. A mother can be cruel. To think the opposite is to give in to outdated views of motherhood and femininity. A mother's cruelty is not always explained by madness. As a woman, and in the name of feminism, I reject that idea, ladies and gentlemen of the jury!'

This last was a bit much, I thought, especially delivered as it was, with a raised fist, but I didn't completely lose confidence in her.

'Evil exists. We would like to believe otherwise, to attribute evil to social inequality, or mental imbalances. That soothes us. We have social services and pills for that. But sometimes, not often, granted, but sometimes evil is just there: the dark side of humanity in all its purity. Evil mothers exist. There are mothers who believe that their children are their creations. Following this perverse logic, they believe they have the right to destroy their own creations. The world, after all, won't change. The harmony of the universe won't be disrupted. They grant themselves that divine right. This is undoubtedly what is going on in Alice's case.'

For the first time in the whole trial, Alice started doodling on the paper in front of her. Her lawyer whispered something in her ear and she stopped what she was doing. Unfortunately, from the sixth row I couldn't make out her scribble.

'Wickedness is so vast,' continued the prosecutor in her sharp voice, 'that it leaves no room for remorse. Few times in my career have I come across such cruelty. Because on top of her cruelty, you have to include her indifference.'

She played it well, better than in the other sessions. She gave rein to her own rage, that much was clear.

Carmela Basaguren asked for an acquittal immediately, citing again Article 20.1 of the Penal Code. Was what Alice did so terrible? She could hardly imagine anything more horrific. Was it unacceptable that this had happened to these children, who deserved all the protection and love in the world? Absolutely. But was it justifiable to lock up this insane, confused, broken woman for the rest of her life? What purpose would that serve? Would the jury really feel they were doing the right thing if they turned in a verdict of guilty? Could they go home to hug their own children with a clear conscience? Would they feel closer to some abstract ideal of justice by failing to consider the circumstances of the case and throwing the accused into a black hole to be forgotten forever? Did she really have to remind us what those circumstances were? Fine. In a nutshell: Alice's depression, her hallucinations, her paranoia, her sudden acts of violence, her utter lack of control over her actions. Whatever their decision, Alice would have to live the rest of her life with the memory of what she had done. And with permanent reminders of the children: their photos, their tiny clothes, their cribs. Smells. Smells are never forgotten. And no jury would ever be able to change that, lighten that load.

Alice rose then to make her final statement and spoke her simple words automatically, while the public and even the judge held their breath.

'I hope to see my babies again someday. I will beg their forgiveness then. It makes no sense to do it here.'

The judge didn't send her back to her seat immediately, but waited a few seconds to see if she had anything more to add. More than a few of us thought she might burst into tears, but that didn't happen. That was it.

'The accused may return to her seat.'

Then the judge turned to the jury. He reminded them of their duty, and recommended that they take their time. Two jurors started to rise, but the judge told them they were not yet free to go.

And so the trial ended. Not with a bang, but a whimper.

I was nervous leaving the chamber, there were too many people, too much sweat. I was hardly thinking about what a letdown the final session had been. There was no climax, but I didn't care. I had something else on my mind. The time would come later to organise what we heard today, tomorrow, or the next day, or the day after that.

But right now I have a date.

Or at least I think I do. I hope I do. But I don't see him, dammit, where is he? I'll wait for him at the exit, but if we don't see each other, I don't have his number, what will I do, but there he is, yes, it's him, calm down, be cool, here he comes, yes, that's better, I'll pretend I didn't see him, I should take out my phone, no, no, he's smiling at me, he's waving, I'll wave back, maybe with a small smile, but take it easy, be cool, nothing to worry about, how's it going, hi, well, it's over, yes, over and done with, what do you say, shall we go for lunch, for lunch, yes, okay, let's go, you'll have to decide where, I don't know this area very well.

5

WAITING FOR THE VERDICT

*I remember moments of peace when for some reason
it was possible to go to the bathroom alone.*
ADRIENNE RICH, *OF WOMAN BORN*

AND EVERYTHING HAPPENED PRETTY MUCH THE WAY I HAD imagined it. Because Jakes did know the area, and suggested a Japanese restaurant two hundred yards from the court building, and when he asked me if I liked Asian food, I said yes, of course, I had lived in London and always went for Asian food there, a pad thai one day, miso soup the next, since that was the cheapest option in an expensive city. In London, eh? What were you doing there? And we moved into comfortable territory on our sweet way to the restaurant.

Until we got to that damned stop light, then, everything was going the way I had imagined it would and I was happy and everything was possible. Since the light was red and I was nervous again, I remembered my phone, which had been on silent all morning, and I had the bright idea to take it out of my handbag, a stupid impulse, almost a tic. Before I even looked at the screen, I knew something wasn't right. And there it was: seven missed calls, three from the nursery, the next four from Niclas. Also a message, a short one, from the father of my child:

'Call me as soon as you can.'

The light turned green then, but I didn't move. I didn't even see Jakes' face, surely registering some confusion. I shut up the little voice inside me that was telling me to throw the phone under the wheels of a car, and called Niclas in order to bring the speeding train of my imagination to a screeching halt.

'Don't panic, but I'm at the hospital with the baby. Something's wrong with him. He has a high fever and he's too drowsy, I can't rouse him.'

Don't panic, the man says. Dammit. But I did panic. A lot. So much so that I got tunnel vision as I said goodbye, goodbye, goodbye, I have to go now, to Jakes, and ran for the car. So much so that I burst into tears when my mother called as I was leaving Gasteiz. She had heard from my father and wanted to check in with me, see how serious it was, ask cautiously if she should buy a plane ticket, but I couldn't tell her much, I didn't know much, there was something wrong with the baby, high fever, stiff neck, they had to do tests, and I was far away, I wasn't there, with him, I was at a trial, no, worse, I was about to have lunch with an attractive man, and I had to hang up, I'd call her later, when we knew more.

And in the 40 miles that separated me from my city, I had time to think a lot of things, and they were all ugly and dark and full of guilt and fear.

ULURU.
Dingo.
Rhodesia.

Alaska.

San Pelayo paediatric ward at Basurto Hospital.

What if that was the final entry?

THE DOCTOR IS A PROFESSIONAL, BUT ALSO WANTS YOU TO know that she's made of flesh and bone.

The doctor doesn't want you to panic, but also doesn't want to give you false hope.

The doctor wants you to understand all the aspects of the situation, but doesn't want to use words that are too complicated.

The doctor is in a hurry, because she has a lot of patients waiting for her, and she's tired because she's been on call for too many damn hours.

The doctor asks you when the child started feeling ill, and you want to tell her that you noticed he felt a bit hot that morning. But, you can't say that to the doctor. How can you tell her you suspected he had a fever but you pretended not to notice, he often has a low-grade fever but it's just a runny nose, the next day he wakes up fine and there's not a thing wrong with him. How do you explain that you filled a thermos flask with lentils for him as always, took him to the nursery as always, stripped him down to his onesie and abandoned him in the arms of the nursery staff as always? How can you tell her that you had considered the possibility that he might be ill, you did know that was a possibility, but you thought, well, if he still has a fever in the afternoon, I'll take him to the paediatrician, but right now I really have to go. How to explain that you gave yourself permission to have your phone on silent all morning? How to explain to the woman in hospital whites about Jade, Alice, the twins, the tub, the trial, the last session, Jakes, the story that was going to come to a nice neat end?

But it didn't.

It didn't end at the trial because it was going to end here.

There was no climax because I had to be here as spectator and party responsible for the climax.

Here in this hallway.

In the saddest hallway in the world.

Have I learnt nothing?

I'll have to learn now. This is the ultimate lesson.

What does a mother have to do, after all? Nose around trials, read poetry, have lunch in Asian restaurants with dark-haired strangers?

No.

A mother has to suffer.

Kneel before the cross and weep.

That is where her destiny is met.

In the place called Golgotha.

Mater dolorosa, mater lacrimosa.

But the doctor speaks, offering a breathing space, something to hold onto, an alibi for the future.

'It's normal that he would have been fine in the morning. Meningitis can develop very quickly.'

And then, to dissolve the echo of that word:

'We're just waiting for the test results now. Don't panic.'

The jury retires to deliberate.

ERIK IS THIN, HE ALWAYS HAS BEEN. HE'S NEVER HAD PLUMP thighs for pinching. At almost fourteen months old, he has almost no hair. When we're out, people rarely tell me he's cute, they say he has the face of an adult, the face of a child, and then, as if they've said something bad, they add 'beautiful eyes' to compensate. But in that hospital cot, red-cheeked and with his sole lock of hair plastered to his forehead, sleeping like an angel thanks to the fever reducers, I realise again that he is perfect.

To me, he is perfect.

Unfortunately, he is also my Achilles heel, an obvious weakness.

On online forums, some mothers write that since they became mothers, they're stronger, invincible, lionesses, all claws and roars. But I've never felt weaker since I became a mother. It's so easy to hurt me now, to sink me, to blow me up. I have a bullseye painted on my forehead. The whole world knows where to strike.

So what are those internet mums talking about? I don't understand. Like them, I feel the same instinct to protect my child, the biological mandate and the conscious desire, and if I have to roar, I'll roar, and if I have to use my claws, I'll use them. But at the same time, I also know that I am impotent in the face of misfortune, I've never been so impotent; my claws, my roars are of little value in a car accident, against a kidnapper, in a fire, against leukaemia, against streptococcus. I am as lost as I've ever been, and weaker than I've ever been.

I felt a pain deep inside when the long needle pierced Erik's tiny spine. I had to look away. Niclas held me.

THE VERDICT HAS ARRIVED. THE LUMBAR PUNCTURE CONFIRMED that it was viral meningitis. In theory, not serious. We could breathe. A prize, perhaps another prize I didn't deserve. A cry for attention. The policeman who gives you a warning instead of a fine. *But don't do it again, you hear?*

Even so, we spent the night at the hospital for observation, they wanted to keep an eye on his fever. I called my mother, who said again she would jump on a plane if necessary, but I told her we had everything under control. I'll never know if she really meant to come or not. Niclas and I spent the night in the armchairs on either side of the cot, forming a Bethlehem portal. We didn't sleep. Erik did, waking only once to feed. We talked from time to time, about any silly thing. The words sweetened the night, made us forget how uncomfortable we were.

Sometimes Erik coughed and we fell silent. Then he'd turn over and go back to sleep, and we'd go back to our conversation. He still smelled like a newborn, but the smell was weaker now, and in a few months, it would be just a memory.

'We're doing alright,' said Niclas.

'We'll do better from now on.'

What I really wanted to say was *I'll do better*.

Niclas fell asleep too, in the end. Sitting as he was, with his neck twisted, his snores sounded funny. He looked like a child. I had two children's sleep to watch over now. I felt totally alone.

Morning came. Erik wasn't feeling any better. He just wanted to be held, and didn't ask to be put down like he always did, he had lost all his desire to explore. We had to wait for the paediatrician. It was a different doctor, who just said what they had said before: there was no treatment, we just had to wait. But if the child still felt ill and his fever didn't come down, we'd have to stay another night. It was a disappointment. We hated the doctor. Our anxiety rose again. It felt like a cheap trick in a low-budget film. At the last minute, when it seems like everything is going well, the final blow falls and fate sneers. A thief of a certain age, pulling off one last job against his will before he retires ... gets caught by the police. The soldier who volunteers for a suicide mission the day before he finishes his tour of duty. The patient who dies half an hour before receiving his discharge papers.

I was eager to get home, ready to start being the perfect mother. But instead, I went home empty-handed, and had a shower and changed clothes in wretched silence. In the evening, Niclas went home to sleep (I insisted), and I prepared to spend a second night at the hospital. In an observation room, alone (fortunately, there were no other children there), you begin to think about everything to the rhythm of your son's deep breathing: convulsions, sudden death, the increasingly credible suspicion that the doctor hasn't told you the whole truth. The second night was the worst. I found no solace in anything. But that night too came to an end and, after the paediatrician's visit, the three of us were free to go home at last. I could hardly breathe until we were out on the street.

We took the tram home, a lucky family who had escaped Herod's massacre unharmed. Erik shouted happily, practising his two words – *Mama! Mama! Mama! Bye-bye! Bye-bye! Bye-bye!* – making some of the other passengers smile. Between the stops on Uribitarte and Pío Baroja, my phone rang, though it was nearly out of battery. I didn't recognise the number and I wasn't going to answer – I'd had enough of that dreadful device – but in the end I answered out of habit.

'Hello, it's Jakes! Where are you? You missed the verdict!'

JAKES WAS INTRIGUED BY ME, ALL THE MORE SO SINCE MY desertion. Truth be told, my face had been familiar to him from the beginning. In the end, he had asked a co-worker from the Ministry of Culture, they had exchanged information, and between the two of them, they figured out who I was. The Ministry of Culture employee had my number from a long-ago interview and gave it to Jakes. The fact that I had not returned to court seemed like a good excuse to call me. After that none too short explanation, he told me what had happened.

'Exemption from criminal responsibility, can you believe it?'

No, I couldn't believe it.

'What?'

'Guilty, but she won't be going to jail.'

'Impossible.'

'We're still waiting to hear what the judge will give her instead of prison time. Oh, sorry, I didn't ask if you're okay, you left in such a hurry the other day.'

'Yes, everything's okay, but I have to go now. I'll call you.'

We got off the tram and Niclas asked with a glance who had called. But I didn't want to say anything, not because I didn't want to mention Jakes, but because I was the mother of a fourteen-month-old recovering from viral meningitis, as simple as that. Nothing else mattered.

AT HOME, WE GOT ERIK SETTLED FOR A NAP AND ORDERED SUSHI. I turned on the television while we were eating, even though Niclas hates that. I assumed the news would open with Alice's trial, but it didn't. It was the fourth or fifth item, and quite brief besides. The woman on trial for killing her son and daughter had been found guilty, but her insanity defence had been accepted. A few images from the courtroom. Alice with a blank stare, hands folded. A brief statement from Carmela Basaguren, expressing moderate satisfaction while they waited for the judge's decision.

Niclas wasn't paying attention, and we didn't talk about the case.

At that moment, I was reevaluating my situation. I had two thousand euros and a bit in my account. Three months to finish my book. A whole lifetime to forget what Alice had done and what the jury had decided.

HYPOTHESIS A

When you are overwhelmed by your fears to such an extent that you manifest them, thinking that you'll regain control of the situation that way. Shock therapy, taken to the extreme. Obsessed with the fragility of the twins' lives, the only way for Alice to free herself of that obsession was to do what frightened her the most: look her fear right in the eye and go for it.

HYPOTHESIS B

When you've achieved everything too easily, you destroy what you've achieved because you don't believe you deserve it, or because you don't value it. This hypothesis explains both the events and the aborted exhibition of Alice's paintings. Additionally, by then she was already an expert at destroying her past and starting from scratch, as demonstrated by the death of Jade. The self-destructive power of the egocentric-capitalist slogan of the self-made (wo)man.

HYPOTHESIS C

Postpartum psychosis, the culmination of a series of undiagnosed mental illnesses. A hypothesis that explains everything using a scientific vocabulary, and without any need for further explanation.

HYPOTHESIS D

As Uncle Ben said, with great power comes great responsibility. While the wisdom of Spiderman's uncle is correct, the reverse can also be said; that is, with great responsibility comes great power. Everyone who has held a new life in their arms has felt that responsibility, but also that power. And that power, for some, is irresistible. (Uncle Ben's statement, by the way, was declared by Roosevelt in April of 1945, shortly before his death, as the United States was preparing to destroy Japan.)

HYPOTHESIS E

Conspiracy. A plot for four hands, concocted by the husband and wife out of a desire to return to their childless life. It's not that hard to imagine that two psychopaths could marry each other and carry out such a life-and-death project. Once they learnt that life with children was not what they had expected, they put their plans into action: the mother's reputation as conflicted and depressive, the father almost always absent. Society itself will decide that the murders are pardonable.

HYPOTHESIS A REQUIRES A TRAGIC HEROINE: CHILDHOOD OF abandonment, troubled adolescence, a destiny marked since birth. A half-psychological, half-mythological approach. Hypothesis B requires a sociological explanation, a discussion of social class issues, perhaps to the point of citing Marx ('material conditions determine consciousness' and so forth ...). Hypothesis C is the objective response of science, the unappealable truth, a favourite hypothesis of jurors but one that falls short as literature. To understand Hypothesis D, we could mention a Basque film that exists now only in the imagination of the elderly (yes, it's an old film, from 1983), *The Death of Mikel*, with its omnipotent and heartless mother. Hypothesis E is best described as a *roman noir*, the one that would give me the best shot at a best seller.

Most likely, the truth, or what we want to call the truth, can be found only by mixing Hypotheses A, B, C, D and E together at unknown doses.

Literature is alchemy.

THE FOLLOWING IS A SHORT BUT NOTABLE PASSAGE FROM AN interview with Carmela Basaguren by Jakes Ruiz de Infante on my birthday (and Sylvia Plath's), 27 October:

Q: You've expressed your satisfaction, not only regarding this case, but also with respect to future cases as well. What do you mean by that?

A: I truly believe that this case represents a critical juncture, and that it will be a point of departure for society as a whole to reflect on mental illness and how it's handled by the penal system. The system's lack of preparation to date is striking, and I don't mean just in terms of resources, though of course, yes, resources; but above all the lack of sensitivity and foresight has been astonishing. It's as if psychiatrists and judges were playing Hot Potato: what to do with the mentally ill when they commit crimes? Until now, as I said, improvisation has reigned supreme, everything depends on the day. Because of its particular characteristics and its prominence in the media, I believe that this case will actually change things.

Q: Following the jury's decision, the judge opted for alternative sentencing, psychiatric treatment instead of jail, but it will be outpatient treatment in this case. Alice Espanet won't even be admitted to a psychiatric hospital.

A: Yes, that's correct. The judge was very clever when it came to plugging the hole in the system. There are only two penitentiary psychiatric hospitals in the whole country, both far from here, in Alicante and Seville, if you can believe that. If Alice were admitted to either one of those, it would place undue inconvenience on her family. Besides, in this case, all the conditions are favourable for outpatient treatment to go well: Alice's good economic situation, her husband's support ... The various institutions will be watching as Alice's treatment progresses until she's fully rehabilitated.

Q: Excuse me, but... are you saying that Alice Espanet received a favourable sentence because of her social status?

A: I said nothing of the sort!

6
ALCHEMY

I am life, and everything I touch will be alive.
ARANTXA URRETABIZKAIA, *WHY LITTLE DARLING*

LITERATURE IS ALCHEMY. PRESCIENTIFIC, BARBARIAN, MYSTIC, rational, emotional, utopian, political, cold, hot, crazy, beautiful, terrible, rhythmic, chaotic, tiresome, ugly, invigorating knowledge. A mystery. One that needs no answers here and now, because it asks me no questions. I write and everything finds its place. Each letter. Each breath. Each sigh.

'Say bye-bye to Mummy!' says my mother every morning with Erik already strapped into his seat. And the little fellow says 'bye-bye, bye-bye.' He's happy to go with this grandmother he only just met. My mother looks happy too. And Niclas is happy, grabbing his surfboard as he rushes out the door, fleeing without even taking the time to give me a kiss. And, above all, I am happy to be alone in my mother's house, having fled inside. Everything is perfect: the temperature, the smell, the murmur of the ocean and the rhythm of the keys. Everyone will come back in two or three hours. Erik asleep, exhausted after playing amongst the volcanic rocks; my mother struck with the awe and wonder of one who has looked under the shell of a child for the first time; Niclas, nose peeling and smelling like a wild thing, blonder than ever.

This perfection has an expiry date that fast approaches, of course. Another six days and we'll have to return to the real world. In six days, my mother will say goodbye with relief and reclaim her sweet solitude, satisfied with the gift she gave us but determined not to do it again any time soon. Then I'll have to take another look at the state of my bank account. I'll have to prepare myself immediately to return to salaried work. And above all: I'll have to read all the pages I've left behind, a violent and disagreeable chore. For Alice will still be there, and the twins, and the ghost of Sylvia Plath and that of her son who committed suicide, Australia will still be there, and Rhodesia, the place called Golgotha, the wound of the woman who has just given birth, and the green plastic tub. Everything will be there and perhaps I will discover that, though I thought I could give it form, it all melted like a frozen statue as soon as I turned my icy gaze away.

In the sun of Lanzarote.

In the middle of a puddle, soaking wet, will be the dark side of my power, my responsibility, watching me, holding me accountable.

Yes, *that* responsibility. Because for a moment, or for several, I put myself in her place. I was those hands. The hands that drowned the babies. The mother's hands. The hands that had no mercy. Because for a moment, or for several, I came to understand what she did, or because I led people to believe that I understood, or because I thought and implied that I could come to understand (why so many twists and turns if not because I am led by the idea that I might find an exit?), and because I wanted to bring you too to that muddy land. Then I returned to this side of the world, to the clean world of love and beautiful words, to the world of mothers who give you plane tickets, to the universe of mothers who sing your child to sleep with the song of the Seven Little Goats three times in a row, to nights of mothers who have recaptured satisfying and half-dirty sex with their surfer husband, to the innocent secrets of mothers who continue writing messages from time to time to a dark-haired journalist. I returned, but I was no longer the same, and I wanted you to not be the same as well, I wanted you to be as muddy as I was in that invisible internal corner.

That is my responsibility. My power. My guilt. My impulse.

Because I have to talk about that muddy territory. It is neither a moral obligation nor a social accusation. It is something much more basic. The muddy land is there, as Everest is there, irresistible. Especially for those of us who are like me.

Defective. We are defective. I am. Would I live better some other way, without this awkward impulse that drives me to seek the most fitting adjective for a murderous mother? Would everything be easier if I didn't have to spend my hours, my best years, on this whole exercise? Would I be happier playing with what others create, enjoying moments, suffering moments, forgetting moments, remembering moments, without thinking about how to put it into words later? I suspect that the answer is yes, but it doesn't matter because impulses cannot be freely chosen. Create, destroy. Sometimes I have to be a monster, bolt the door, get my hands dirty, get others muddy. Rarely.

What I did, I did for myself. Following my own impulse to the last comma. But I'd like to think I also did it for the twins. Let them taste at least a tiny bit of what was denied them. After all, I am life. And at the end of the day, I try to banish death.

For their help, I would like to thank Ibone Olza, María Ramos, Lizar Aguirre, Virginia Senosiain, Harkaitz Cano, Amaia Agirre, Aixa de la Cruz and all those who took care of my children while I was writing.

TABLE OF CONTENTS

KATIXA AGIRRE (GASTEIZ - EUSKADI, 1981)

I started writing short stories and reading them to my classmates at a very young age, just for fun, and for some reason I thought this was something everybody did. It was not until the age of fifteen that I started winning literary contests at school and began taking it a bit more seriously. I published my first short story book in 2007 and I haven't stopped since.

In my case, I had to stand at a peculiar crossroads. In fact, every bilingual Basque writer has to do this. Do I write in one of the major languages in which I live (depending on which side of the border you live that would be French or Spanish) or do I choose Basque, a minority language, as my literary language? Basque literature is a relatively new addition to world literature. Being the literature of a minority culture, Basque literature and us authors face interesting and, in some cases, unique questions that not only shape the stories that have been produced but help interpret the context in which Basque literature has developed. I never regretted choosing this small language. I know I have a potentially much smaller audience. However, translations from Basque are becoming more and more frequent – my own work has been already translated into ten languages.

For me it's been an absolute pleasure when my novels have been translated and read abroad. That such a thing can happen, and that the world can be united in that tiny way through a book, amazes me.

KRISTIN ADDIS HAS WORKED FOR SOME THIRTY YEARS AS A translator. She translates primarily between Spanish or Basque and English, and is one of few who translate directly from Basque into English. She specialises in literary translation, which she especially enjoys, and has translated short stories, novels, and poetry. She has also translated various works about the Basque language and culture. Ms Addis has spent many years in the Basque Country; she currently resides in Iowa with her family.

We translate female authors who write in minority languages. Only women. Only minority languages. This is our choice.

We know that we only win if we all win, that's why we are proud to be fair trade publishers. And we are committed to supporting organisations in the UK that help women to live freely and with dignity.

We are 3TimesRebel.